ENDORSEMENTS

"John Grace is to be congratulated on his short investment primmer. If you just read the snappy section titles, you'll become so interested that you will read this fast moving book. I am sure that many will find great wisdom in John's forty years of learned experiences. As they say, experience is the great teacher."

—Lacy H. Hunt, Economist, Ph.D.

"I first came to know John Grace in 1999 when he became Master Certified and a Charter Member here at Dent Research. John has taken what he has studied and earned over the last 20 years and has written an easy to read and implement strategies that apply to all investors, those who are just starting out as well as those who are inspired to maintain their balances, no matter what the markets might do. John is spot on when he says, "It's not about the prediction, it's all about the preparation.""

—Harry Dent, bestselling author
and renowned economic forecaster,
Founder & President, Dent Research

"As a mother of a beautiful daughter with special needs and a practicing physician for 15 years, I highly recommend this informative and interesting book to help us all better plan for our financial futures. John Grace expertly explains the recent factors that are influencing our economy and provides a historical context in which to help guide decisions about investments. We all share a common desire to be financially secure in our future. This book provides a timely discussion of how best to prepare in these uncertain times."

—Carolyn Flynn DO, Family Practice Hospitalist in
Winchester, VA

"Independent thinking is precious among investment managers precisely because it's so rare. John Grace is one of those independent thinkers you should listen to. In Making Finance Make Sense, John drills down to what really drives the economy and the financial markets and gives his outlook for the years ahead. Ignore his words at your peril."

—Charles Lewis Sizemore, CFA

"As a business attorney, I found John's book to be well written with lots of very interesting and thoughtful information. John's concepts are thoroughly researched and they provide strong reasoning for his comments and conclusions. I also appreciate his underlying theme; Hope for the best as you plan for the worse. His historical perspective and thoughts about the future provide food for thought too."

—Patrick L. Garofalo, Esq.

"I have been traveling back and forth between Argentina and the U.S. for more than a decade. Now 31, married, and a father, the world has suddenly become very scary. The concepts in this book are clear, simple to follow, and backed up by solid research and deep analysis, rather than unqualified opinions or guessing. I recommend it to anyone trying to understand what's behind all of the financial noise we hear everyday and for those planning for the long term rather than a quick win. In fact, my wife and I now know, for example, why it was so difficult for us to find a store that carried diapers for our 1 year old when we travelled to Italy for a wedding. We now have our strategies in place and a clear roadmap, so we feel confident about the next decades, no matter how the market turns. Thanks to putting this book to work our plans are in place whether we live to 100 or die tomorrow."

—Fernando Florez

So Michael,
let's be amazing!
JG

MAKING FINANCE
MAKE SENSE

STRIVING TO WIN

JOHN GRACE

JONES MEDIA
PUBLISHING

Making Finance Make Sense: Striving to Win Copyright © 2020 by John Grace.

AUM Disclaimer:
IAC is part of The Elite Financial Network in Huntington Beach, CA that manages close to $800 million assets under management, according to Dan Cairo, Registered Principal, 10/23/19.

Disclaimer:

The author strives to be as accurate and complete as possible in the creation of this book, notwithstanding the fact that the author does not warrant or represent at any time that the contents within are accurate due to the rapidly changing nature of the Internet.

While all attempts have been made to verify information provided in this publication, the Author and Publisher assume no responsibility and are not liable for errors, omissions, or contrary interpretation of the subject matter herein. The Author and Publisher hereby disclaim any liability, loss or damage incurred as a result of the application and utilization, whether directly or indirectly, of any information, suggestion, advice, or procedure in this book. Any perceived slights of specific persons, peoples, or organizations are unintentional.

In practical advice books, like anything else in life, there are no guarantees of income made. Readers are cautioned to rely on their own judgment about their individual circumstances to act accordingly. Readers are responsible for their own actions, choices, and results. This book is not intended for use as a source of legal, business, accounting or financial advice. All readers are advised to seek services of competent professionals in legal, business, accounting, and finance field.

Printed in the United States of America

ISBN: 978-1-945849-88-6 paperback
JMP2020.8

Contents

INTRODUCTION

Americans are wildly optimistic about what it takes to make work optional. And the securities industry isn't helping much at all. With 40 years of experience (not repeating the first year 40 times) I have accepted the challenge to make a difference and make sense.

Opinions are like belly buttons: everybody has one. What I am offering here is a collection of informed opinions. General George S. Patton hit the nail on the head with his observation, "If everyone is thinking alike, then somebody isn't thinking."

Speaking of not thinking, almost 60% of Americans fantasize that $1 million will be enough for "a comfortable retirement," according to TD Ameritrade's 2019 Retirement Pulse Survey. 1015 U.S. adults ages 23 and older with at least $10,000 in investable assets were surveyed.[1]

While $1 million is a popular perspective about what it takes to retire comfortably, that amount may not be enough for you and your family. Whether you're planning a vacation, a wedding, or retirement you *have* to do the math. Here is where I think the Navy Seal motto adopted from a 2010 album fits in perfectly. "The only easy day was yesterday."

Naturally, everyone's situation is different. It's certainly possible to retire with $1 million in savings, and many Americans live on much less, the question that only you can answer is, How much do YOU need?

---

1 "2019 Retirement Pulse Survey." https://s2.q4cdn.com/437609071/files/doc_news/research/2019/retirement-pulse-survey.pdf. 2019. PDF File.

I earned my life and disability license in 1978 and my first securities license in 1979. So, according to me, I am well qualified to apologize for how the insurance industry can lead investors astray, along with how the securities industry disappoints investors, too often leaving you high and dry.

Investors today are unfocused and delusional. On the one hand investors love it when they make money and hate it when they lose. But savvy investors hate losses more than they love gains. We will peel back the onions so you can see what you can do, whether you live too long or die too soon.

For five years my firm paid $10,000 a year for objective research. I can tell you when I pay that kind of money for information I read everything. Then I read it again. Let me put it in perspective. I was at a family party around the holidays when my 11 year old niece who love math, out of the blue, came over and asked me to tell her how the economy works in one sentence.

As I scoured the room looking for the adult who put Nicole up to this task I said, "My best answer about how the economy works is to study the ordinary buying behavior of consumers **BASED ON AGE**."

Here's a simple example that will make you chuckle. You probably didn't notice that you consumed the most potato chips in life around age 14. Nor did you notice the pattern when you were a 41 year old parent you purchased the most potato chips in your life for your 14 year old(s).

Here's another one for you. Young family friends from Argentina went to Italy for a wedding in 2018 and were astonished to find how difficult it was to buy diapers there for their 1 year old. How could that possibly be? Here's my best answer. There are more people older than 65 than younger than 5 for the first time ever, per Markets Insider, February 20, 2019.

This is unchartered territory. Everything has just changed. You see, the world's population is aging while many countries' birth rates fail to keep up. Include the U.S. here.[2]

So, let me encourage you to read here what I think is one of the best resources you now have in your hands. Please keep in mind our company trademark, "The proof is in the planning."

---

2 Markets Insider. 20 Feb. 2019. https://markets.businessinsider.com/news

1

U.S. Growth Thanks to Debt, Not D.C.

My audience may remember how early 2018 I referenced Jeffrey Gundlach, chief executive officer at DoubleLine Capital for saying he believed the market would gain 15 percent before finishing in the red. He certainly called the loss for the year. I enjoyed the opportunity to meet Gundlach in Carlsbad, CA late February this year at a forum for financial advisers where I acknowledged him for the great call. I follow Gundlach for a number of reasons. He is known to be a billionaire in his own right, he oversees more than $130 billion in assets at the firm, according to Yahoo Finance, and he is definitely his own man. Which means, he doesn't have hierarchy dictating to him that he must constantly beat the drum that everything is just fine, because no matter what, it's always stocks for the long haul.[3]

Gundlach's remarks in his investor webcast on May 14, 2019, are particularly noteworthy. You will see that his observations mirror my own. President Donald Trump began declaring, and repeated often since then that, "We have the 'greatest economy'" ever on Fox News, October 16, 2018. And a lot of people back up his claim. But some observers see things vastly different.[4]

In his webcast, Gundlach said that U.S. growth is derived "exclusively" from government, mortgage, and corporate debt. In fact, had it not been for the debt increase the economy would have already contracted. "Nominal GDP

3 "DoubleLine's Gundlach says new U.S. tariffs on China likely." https://finance.yahoo.com/news/doublelines-gundlach-says-u-tariffs-173249134.html. Reuters, Yahoo Finance 2019. Web. 7 May 2019.
4 Trish Reagan . "Interview: Trish Regan of Fox Business News Interviews Donald Trump." 2018. Video

growth over the past five years would have been negative if U.S. public debt had not increased," said Gundlach. "One thing everybody seems to miss when they look at these GDP numbers ... they seem to not understand that the growth in the GDP it looks pretty good on the screen is really based exclusively on debt – government debt, also corporate debt and even now some growth in mortgage debt," said Gundlach.

"If those non-Treasury debt categories had not grown, either, GDP would have been very negative," Reuters reported May 15, 2019, from an email following the webcast. Had the U.S. Treasury avoided increasing its debt then nominal GDP would have been negative in three of the last five years, Gundlach opined, "even with all of the exact mortgage, corporate, and student loan growth that occurred." He really drove home his point with the math. He asserts nominal GDP growth was 4.3 percent, but that is more than offset by the 4.7 percent growth in total public debt.[5]

Gundlach said again that he doesn't see the U.S. headed into recession anytime soon, but there are some weaknesses showing up in the U.S. economy. Against the debt drama and Wall Street "addicted to Federal Reserve stimulus," these are "very, very dangerous times" for the next U.S. recession. He went on to point out the Citi Economic Data Change Index released May 15, 2019, which has fallen to its lowest level since the financial crisis.[6]

Meanwhile, thanks to softer rhetoric by President Trump who, according to me, seems motivated to keep stock losses at 5 percent or less, there are fresh woes over fears Italy's fiscal situation after Rome said it could break EU fiscal rules to spur employment contends Reuters In a separate May 15, 2019, article. And then there's

5 "Core Fixed Income & Flexible Income." https:// doublelinefunds.com/webcasts/#. Jeffrey Gundlach, 2019 2019. Web. 14 May 2019.
6 "Core Fixed Income & Flexible Income." https:// doublelinefunds.com/webcasts/#. Jeffrey Gundlach, 2019 2019. Web. 14 May 2019.

China data revealing surprising weak retail sales and industrial output growth.[7]

The good news is investors don't need to see the future to prepare for it. For all the "monetary central planning, financial engineering, political lily-gilding can't hold back the forces of creative destruction forever," David Stockman wrote to subscribers May 15, 2019. So, by analogy, we all know that football teams typically have eleven men on offense as well as the exact same number of players on defense. To be prepared for the good, the bad, and the unforeseen in 2019, now is the time for investors to develop your defensive strategies.[8]

7 "DoubleLine's Gundlach says new U.S. tariffs on China likely." https://finance.yahoo.com/news/doublelines-gundlach-says-u-tariffs-173249134.html. Reuters, Yahoo Finance 2019. Web. 7 May 2019.
8 "When The Wall Street Chart-Monkeys Become Whirling Dervishes---It's Time For A Plan On How Not To Become COLLATERAL DAMAGE." https://davidstockmanscontracorner.com/when-the-wall-street-chart-monkeys-become-whirling-dervishes-its-time-for-a-plan-on-how-not-to-become-collateral-damage/. David Stockman, Contra Corner 2019. Web. 15 May 2019.

2

YOU CAN'T READ THE ECONOMY BY THE HEADLINES

As we celebrate a ten-year-old bull market it is worthwhile to see how we got here. Yogi Berra called it correctly with his statement, "It's tough to make predictions, especially about the future." At a press conference on March 3, 2009, it was at the time President Obama who said, "What you're now seeing is profit and earning rations are starting to get to the point where buying stocks is a potentially good deal if you've got a long term perspective on in." The stock market hit its low point less than a week later on March 9, 2009. On that day the S&P 500 closed at 676. The S&P 500 closed at 2743 on March 8, 2019, which makes for a 306 percent gain, according to Yahoo Finance.[9]

The president also expressed optimism that hiring and business investment would pick up. But it wasn't until June 2014, over five years after the president's high hopes for hiring that the economy fully recovered all the jobs lost during the Great Recession, according to CNN Business, March 9, 2015.[10]

We begin the 11th year of a bull market with the market opening on March 11, 2019. The date is interesting on a couple of fronts. First, President Donald Trump proposed a record $4.7 trillion federal budget for 2020 on Monday. This president is counting on an optimistic 3.1 percent economic growth projections, along with accounting adjustments, and steep domestic cuts to balance future spending in 15 years. Trump's argument is that the nation is experiencing "an economic miracle." While the

9 Yahoo Finance. 2019. 2019. Web. 8 March 2019
10 https://www.cnn.com/business. 2015. Web. 9 March 2015.

national debt is $22 trillion, the deficit is likely to hit $1.1 trillion in fiscal year 2020, the highest in a decade.[11]

Trump is certain the tax cuts will fuel robust growth. Some economists, however, submit the tax cut bump is flattening, as they see slower growth in the coming years. What concerns this observer the most is the piling on of even more debt by this administration with no planned correction.[12]

The second reason the second Monday, March 2019 is notable is there is an increasing number of economists on Wall Street who are downgrading their expectations for U.S. first quarter growth. December's retail figures dropped sharply which may be an indication consumers are losing their enthusiasm for spending.

---

11 "Trump Proposes a Record $4.75 Trillion Budget." https://www.nytimes.com/2019/03/11/us/politics/trump-budget.html. Michael Tackett Jim Tankersley , 2019 2019. Web. 11 March 2019.
12 "The truth about Trump's 'economic miracle'." https://www.bostonglobe.com/opinion/2019/02/07/the-truth-about-trump-economic-miracle/dHaLjfw4y5A5nqv990c3AJ/story.html. Margery Eagan, 2019 2019. Web. 7 Feb 2019.

"The nearly $21 trillion U.S. economy relies heavily on consumer spending, which comprises about ⅔ of gross domestic product," according to yahoo Finance, March 11, 2019.[13]

A number of those who watch the economy have tempered their expectations for growth during the first three months of this year. The Q1 GDP is "tracking very weak," Goldman Sachs opined. Capital Economics suggests that consumer spending "is likely to remain unusually weak in the first quarter." As some suggest overall GDP growth will slow to below 2%, others see softer retail data that GDP could check in at 1.5% in the first quarter. Last month, the Atlanta Federal Reserve forecasted "that fourth quarter 2018 growth would fall under 2 percent, well below the government's initial estimate of 2.7 percent and short of President Donald Trump's

---

13 "Wall Street mulls sub-2% U.S. growth as consumers cut back on spending." https://finance.yahoo.com/news/wall-street-economic-gdp-growth-less-than-2-percent-155133619.html. Javier E. David, Yahoo Finance 2019. Web. 11 March 2019.

self-imposed target of 3 percent," reported Yahoo Finance.[14]

Rather than believing hope is a strategy and optimism is an investment foundation, let me suggest that you review your portfolio expectations. Greg Davis Vanguard Group Chief Investment Officer sees "near 50-50 chance of recession in 2020," said on CNBC February 11. 2019. Davis said further, "Our expectations around U.S. equity markets if for about a 5 percent median, annualized return." Now is the time to do for your portfolio what your car's GPS does when you miss a turn, 'Recalculating...'[15]

---

14 "Wall Street mulls sub-2% U.S. growth as consumers cut back on spending." https://finance.yahoo.com/news/wall-street-economic-gdp-growth-less-than-2-percent-155133619.html. Javier E. David, Yahoo Finance 2019. Web. 11 March 2019.
15 "We're at the high end of fair market value, says Vanguard chief investment officer." https://www.cnbc.com/video/2019/02/11/were-at-the-high-end-of-fair-market-value-says-vanguard-president.html. SQUAWK ALLEY, 2019 2019. Web. 11 Feb 2019.

3

A MILLENNIAL CALAMITY WILL BECOME AMERICA'S BURDEN

It's been said that once we make our habits, then our habits make us. A habit that people who retire well maintain is the practice of deferred gratification. Unfortunately, it appears that Millennials who grew up with everyone on every team getting a trophy every time have developed the habit of getting instant gratification.

Let me begin by making something as clear as I can, that for some reason often blows many people's minds. If your goal in one year, after accounting for Social Security and any pension income, is to receive additional income of $40,000, by using the 4% withdrawal it rule, it means you will need to place $1,000,000 in an account where the yield is 4% today to achieve your goal one year from now. We can all agree that $40,000 isn't a lot of money anymore, and we used to think that being a millionaire made you rich, but things have changed. Remember this is just one year. So, if your goal is sometime in the future, you need to account for inflation.

If you wanted to create an income of $100,000 in a year, simply multiply that goal by 25 to see that the amount invested with a 4% yield is $2,500,000. With pensions becoming history for many workers and Social Security becoming questionable for lots of future retirees, it is clear the job that must be done is the responsibility of those who work for a living. Which means it is vital for each of us to develop good habits that can stand the test of change and time.

Instead of planning for their future, "Nearly 60% of investors 18-34 say they already have taken money from their retirement account," according to research from E-Trade Financial reported Sarah O'Brien, CNBC, August 21, 2018. In addition to carrying most of the $1.4 trillion in college loans, Millennials wages are lower than their parents' income in their 20s: "$40,581 vs. $50,910 (inflation-adjusted) earned by Baby Boomers in 1989," according to a study by advocacy group Young Invincibles in 2017. As you can see in the chart below, the top three reasons identified for the withdrawals are medical emergencies, education costs, and unemployment. Do not miss the fifth reason, to simply spend on myself/family. In fact, 36% made a withdrawal for these reasons; big purchases, vacations or spend it on themselves or family.

Reason for early withdrawal	Under age 34	Ages 35-54	Age 55 & over
For a medical emergency	23%	13%	3%
To pay for education	22%	16%	3%
Because I became unemployed	17%	12%	3%
To make a large purchase	16%	12%	3%
To simply spend on myself/family	13%	6%	1%
To spend on a vacation	7%	1%	1%
Other	1%	3%	3%

Source: E★Trade's StreetWise quarterly study

Wise quarterly study Sarah O'Brien reminds us that withdrawals from a traditional retirement account, before 59 ½ not only generates an income tax bill but, unless one of a few exclusions are met, there is also a 10% early withdrawal penalty. When your Millennial loved one tells you the intention is to put the money back, you need to know that is not likely to happen.[16]

Some of the money might show up again, but the total may not be 100%. More significantly, when $10,000 is removed from the account, the earnings and interest on the original value would be lost over several decades. By example, In spite of 2000-02 and 2007-08, $10,000 invested January 1988 in the S&P 500 index would have been valued at $211,900 by the end of the year 2017, according to the MoneyChimp online calculator. With continued contributions, $200,000 is a good start to help get to what will

---

16 "Majority of young workers have already tapped their retirement savings." https://www.cnbc.com/2018/08/21/millennials-and-early-401k-withdrawals.html. Sarah O'Brien, 2018 2018. Web. 21 Aug 2018.

certainly need to be more than $1,000,000 in the future.[17]

An E-Trade Financial study shows that just as Millennials have increased 401(k) withdrawals by 31% since 2015, the Generation X group has increased withdrawals by 30%, with 45% turning to their 401(ks) for cash. Regardless of what the stock market does, with gaps in employment Millennials will not pay as much as they would have in Social Security. Further, the age of becoming eligible for Social Security benefits may be advanced. They are not likely at all to have a pension.[18]

These are habits that can well contribute to living with a lot less money for life. Unless something changes, the Millennial calamity will become America's burden. Or we can all learn and apply something from our elders. At 90 my

17 "Majority of young workers have already tapped their retirement savings." https://www.cnbc.com/2018/08/21/millennials-and-early-401k-withdrawals.html. Sarah O'Brien, 2018 2018. Web. 21 Aug 2018.
18 "Majority of young workers have already tapped their retirement savings." https://www.cnbc.com/2018/08/21/millennials-and-early-401k-withdrawals.html. Sarah O'Brien, 2018 2018. Web. 21 Aug 2018.

mother who loved being the responsible party for paying her own bills asked me to go online to confirm that her bank balance was in good order.

I was astonished to see that every month she automatically moved money from her checking account to her savings account. I gave my mother a high five because I could not only confirm that her accounts were in good order, but I had to thank her for teaching me to begin early by setting aside allowance money for those rainy days as well as a bright future. Little did I realize that the practice also sowed the seeds for me to become a securities and insurance broker. No regrets.

4

READY FOR A CORRECTION?
PROBABLY NOT.

What it takes to be a successful investor these days can be summarized in four words: bigger gambles, lower returns. It used to be the case that reducing risk was accomplished by holding bonds. Now the job of risk reduction has simply become more complicated.

Former Lehman Brothers analyst Brian Sozzi asked and answered a very important question of investors. " Ready for the stock market correction? Probably not." Sozzi is now a columnist at The Street where the title of his September 11, 2018 article declared (bold added), "Investors Have Learned Squat 10 Years After the Lehman Brothers Bankruptcy."[19]

There are three things we have learned since the Financial Crisis. First, as opposed to the ancient mantra 'Buy & Hold' no matter what, investors can put technology to work to ascertain in advance of the grits hitting the fan how much risk they are willing to accept. Then they can see how their portfolio might be designed to perform within the specific risk parameters. Second, since savvy investors hate losses more than they love gains, many have put strategies into the equation that can move money out of risk assets in a bad year like 2008 to cash to limit losses. The same systems move back into risk assets like 2009 to limit the downside and participate in as much of the upside as possible. The third piece to the puzzle includes learning from the endowments and institutional investors

19 "Investors Have Learned To Squat 10 Years After the Lehman Brothers Bankruptcy." https://www.thestreet.com/investing/investors-have-learned-squat-10-years-after-the-lehman-brothers-bankruptcy-14707453. BRIAN SOZZI, TheStreet 2018. Web. 11 Sep 2018.

by diversifying into more asset classes unlike ever before.

With low interest rates in the U.S., negative rates in in other countries, and lackluster growth, investors have become more creative by embracing increased risk to bolster their performances. Twenty years ago it was possible to earn 7.5% just by owning investment grade bonds. To come close to what is considered a strong return of 7.5%, endowments and pension funds are moving into riskier investments by adding large positions in global stocks, real estate, and private equity investments to the once standard investment of high grade bonds.

In 1995, a portfolio made up wholly of bonds would return 7.5% a year with a likelihood that returns could vary by about 6%, according to research by Callan Associates Inc., which advises large investors. To make a 7.5% return in 2015, Callan found, investors needed to spread money across risky assets, shrinking bonds to just 12% of the portfolio. Private equity and stocks needed to take up some three-quarters of the entire investment pool. But with the added risk, returns could vary by more than 17%, per The Wall Street Journal, May 31, 2016.[20]

Rolling the Dice

Investors grappling with lower interest rates have to take bigger risks if they want to equal returns of two decades ago.

Estimates of what investors needed to earn 7.5%

	1995	2005	2015	
			12%	Bonds
		52%	33%	U.S. Large Cap
			8%	U.S. Small Cap
	100% Bonds	20%	22%	Non-U.S. Equity
		5%		
		14%	13%	Real Estate
		5%	12%	Private Equity
		4%		
Expected return	7.5%	7.5%	7.5%	
Standard deviation*	6.0%	8.9%	17.2%	

*Likely amount by which returns could vary
Source: Callan Associates

THE WALL STREET JOURNAL.

20 "Pension Funds Pile on Risk Just to Get a Reasonable Return." https://www.wsj.com/articles/pension-funds-pile-on-the-risk-just-to-get-a-reasonable-return-1464713013. Timothy W. Martin, The Wall Street Journal 2016. Web. 11 Oct 2019.

In the past bonds produced a source of safe, consistent streams of profit that allowed long-term, risk averse investors to hit annual targets. The era of low rates has all but made that buffer disappear. Investors must now compensate by embracing other bets that could be a home run or a strike-out. The Callan reports highlights how risky an endeavor that is. It also shows to produce the same 7.5% annual return additional diversification is necessary.[21]

This isn't your typical 60% stocks and 40% bonds retail portfolio (or vice versa). Let's look at the smart money as represented by The Yale Endowment, June 2018 annual return (net of fees) 12.3% valued at $29.4 billion.

Asset Allocation

Yale continues to maintain a well-diversified, equity-oriented portfolio, with the following asset allocation targets for fiscal year 2019:

21 "Scotiabank Profit Falls 12%, Hurt by Energy Loans." https://www.wsj.com/articles/scotiabank-profit-falls-12-hurt-by-energy-loans-1464695495?mod=searchresults&page=1&pos=3. Rita Trichur, Ben Dummett, The Wall Street Journal. 2016. Web. 11 Oct 2019.

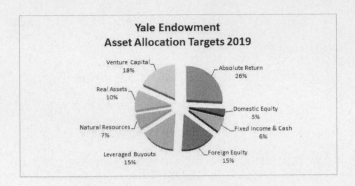

Source: YaleNews October 1, 2018

Three things to take notice here. The first observation that strikes this observer is that Yale has allocated 3.0% to U.S. equities, 6.5% to bonds and cash, and 15.5% to foreign equities, which makes for a total of 25.0% in traditional asset classes. Secondly, when looking at the ratios I am struck by the small bets. The largest position is 26% to Absolute return. Another way to look at it is retail investors have been told you were diversified with a mix of 60% this and 40% that. Clearly, Yale has a different perspective. Finally, where many investors have place 2 or

3 legs under their portfolio stool, Yale counts 8 asset classes.[22]

Please do not read this to be a template for you to follow. But if success leaves clues, and I believe it does, there is a lot to learn from the best and the brightest. It is also interesting to note as compared to its peers, Yale's endowment finds itself in an unfamiliar spot as it came in last in the Ivy League, posting a 5.7% return in fiscal 2019, as Bloomberg News reported September 27, 2019. At the same time, David Swensen, Yale Endowment's CIO took over the job in 1985. "Under his stewardship during the past 34 years the Yale Endowment generated returns of 13.5% per annum, a record unequalled among institutional investors. He leads a staff of 32," per Yale.edu. Yale's endowment was worth $1 billion in 1985 when David Swensen took on the job. Now it's 29 times that, according to Bloomberg News. It would not surprise me to learn that

22 "Investment return of 12.3% brings Yale endowment value to $29.4 billion." https://news.yale.edu/2018/10/01/investment-return-123-brings-yale-endowment-value-294-billion. Karen N. Peart, Yale News 2018. Web. 1 Oct 2018.

Swensen follows the thinking of Mahatma Gandi, "Live as if you were to die tomorrow."[23]

Former analyst, Brian Sozzi now at *The Street* got my attention on September 15, 2018, with his headline "**Investors Have Learned To Squat 10 Years After the Lehman Brothers Bankruptcy**". We can agree that opinions are like belly buttons, everybody has one. But you and I prefer to listen and learn from those with informed opinions, and Brian is certainly well qualified.[24]

It was four years into his Wall Street analyst job on September, 15, 2008 when Brian reflects ," I only thought deep down days in the market were buying opportunities. After all, the old B.S. line on Wall Street for years has been 'buy low, sell high.' Selling dominated my trading screens, high-stakes drama was playing out on

23 "Investment return of 12.3% brings Yale endowment value to $29.4 billion." https://news.yale.edu/2018/10/01/investment-return-123-brings-yale-endowment-value-294-billion. Karen N. Peart, Yale News 2018. Web. 1 Oct 2018.
24 "Investors Have Learned To Squat 10 Years After the Lehman Brothers Bankruptcy." https://www.thestreet.com/investing/investors-have-learned-squat-10-years-after-the-lehman-brothers-bankruptcy-14707453. BRIAN SOZZI, TheStreet 2018. Web. 11 Sep 2018.

business news networks and behind the scenes in DC, and an entire generation of investors were being wiped out — houses, stocks, you name it. But thinking back to that time and today's environment, I can confidently say most investors have learned nothing 10 years since the Lehman bust."[25]

Brian went on to say what may sound very familiar to too many investors, "People are simply riding momentum because everyone else is and they don't know how to read a cash flow statement. Some continue to hold Lehman lessons dear, but it's my view the majority have moved on without revisiting that time every quarter, as they should. It's sad and it will come back to bite investors – again- within the next five years."[26]

---

25 "Investors Have Learned To Squat 10 Years After the Lehman Brothers Bankruptcy." https://www.thestreet.com/investing/investors-have-learned-squat-10-years-after-the-lehman-brothers-bankruptcy-14707453. BRIAN SOZZI, TheStreet 2018. Web. 11 Sep 2018.
26 "Investors Have Learned To Squat 10 Years After the Lehman Brothers Bankruptcy." https://www.thestreet.com/investing/investors-have-learned-squat-10-years-after-the-lehman-brothers-bankruptcy-14707453. BRIAN SOZZI, TheStreet 2018. Web. 11 Sep 2018.

First, let's look at the smart money as represented by The Yale Endowment, June 2017 annual return (net of fees) 11.3%.[27]

Source: Yale Endowment, Investor's Advantage Corp.

This isn't your typical 60 percent stocks and 40 percent bond portfolio. The Asset Allocation report http://investments.yale.edu/ reads "Over the past 30 years, Yale dramatically reduced the Endowment's dependence on domestic marketable securities by reallocating assets to nontraditional asset classes. In 1985, over four-fifths of the Endowment was committed to U.S. stocks, bonds, and cash. Today, domestic marketable securities account for approximately

27 "Investment return of 11.3% brings Yale endowment value to $27.2 billion." https://news.yale.edu/2017/10/10/investment-return-113-brings-yale-endowment-value-272-billion. Tom Conroy, Yale News 2017. Web. 11 October 2019.

one-tenth of the portfolio, while foreign equity, private equity, absolute return strategies, and real assets represent nearly nine-tenths of the Endowment," according to Yale Investments Office.[28]

Further, "The heavy allocation to non-traditional asset classes stems from their return potential and diversifying power. Today's actual and target portfolios have significantly higher expected returns and lower volatility than the 1985 portfolio. Alternative assets, by their very nature, tend to be less efficiently priced than traditional marketable securities, providing an opportunity to exploit market inefficiencies through active management. The Endowment's long time horizon is well suited to exploiting illiquid, less efficient markets such as venture capital, leveraged buyouts, oil and gas, timber, and real estate." In closing, "In 1985, when alternative asset classes accounted for only 12 percent of

28 "Investment return of 11.3% brings Yale endowment value to $27.2 billion." https://news.yale.edu/2017/10/10/investment-return-113-brings-yale-endowment-value-272-billion. Tom Conroy, Yale News 2017. Web. 11 October 2019.

the Endowment, Yale faced a 21 percent chance of a disruptive spending drop, in which real spending drops by 10 percent over two years, and a 36 percent chance of purchasing power impairment, in which real Endowment values fall by 50 percent over fifty years. By 2016, when absolute return, private equity, and real assets accounted for approximately 74 percent of the Endowment, disruptive spending drop risk fell to 8 percent, and purchasing power impairment risk declined to 10 percent."[29]

There is no recommendation in my article here for investors to try and follow Yale's model. But if it is the case that success leaves clues, as I believe it does, there may be some things we can learn from some of the best and the brightest. Yale observed, "The rigor required in conducting mean-variance analysis brings

29 "Investment return of 11.3% brings Yale endowment value to $27.2 billion." https://news.yale.edu/2017/10/10/investment-return-113-brings-yale-endowment-value-272-billion. Tom Conroy, Yale News 2017. Web. 11 October 2019.

an important element of discipline to the asset allocation process."[30]

What I find encouraging is that Yale is doing exceptional work. I am inspired to follow their lead. As opposed to a two asset class composition of 60% stocks and 40% bonds (or vice versa), please do notice Yale holds eight asset classes outside of cash. Please pay particular attention to their holdings by percentage in U.S. equity and fixed income.

It is my opinion that to be better prepared for the good, the bad, and the unforeseen savvy investors will diversify unlike they have ever diversified in the past. According to the Wallstreet Journal, in 1995 a 7.5% return was simply achieved with 100 percent bonds. To achieve the same 7.5 return results in 2005, bonds were 52 percent, US equity 25 percent, real estate 14% and private equity 4%. By 2015, bonds were 12 percent, US equity 41%, non-US

30 "Investment return of 11.3% brings Yale endowment value to $27.2 billion." https://news.yale.edu/2017/10/10/investment-return-113-brings-yale-endowment-value-272-billion. Tom Conroy, Yale News 2017. Web. 11 October 2019.

stocks 22%, real estate 13%, and private equity 12 percent.[31]

Allow me to confess that my peers and I accept responsibility for failing to help investors see how their portfolios may be any better prepared for the approaching storm(s). Perhaps this work will help right our ship before the next disaster reaches your life savings.

---

31 "Pension Funds Pile on Risk Just to Get a Reasonable Return." https://www.wsj.com/articles/pension-funds-pile-on-the-risk-just-to-get-a-reasonable-return-1464713013. Timothy W. Martin, The Wall Street Journal 2016. Web. 11 Oct 2019.

5

RUN FOR COVER

About four years before the 2000–02 "tech wreck" where the NASDAQ dropped 80%, according to Yahoo Finance, former Federal Reserve chairman Alan Greenspan warned of "irrational exuberance" at a dinner speech.[32]

In an interview with CNN on December 17, 20018 Greenspan said, "It would be very surprising to see it (markets) sort of stabilize here, and then take off." Greenspan went on to say leading stock indexes may have a little upside left. But that's only going to make the inevitable

32 "ALAN GREENSPAN: The bull market is over, and investors should 'run for cover'." https://markets.businessinsider.com/news/stocks/stock-market-news-alan-greenspan-warns-investors-to-run-for-cover-2018-12-1027818871. Rebecca Ungarino, 2018 2018. Web. 18 Dec 2018.

drop more painful. So, "at the end of that run, run for cover," he said. Now, I don't know if Greenspan is correct, nor do I offer an opinion as to how much time there might be before a major downturn. I do know that no one needs to foresee the future to prepare for it.[33]

"If everyone is thinking alike, then somebody isn't thinking."
– General George S. Patton

Who told us in 2007 that Credit Default Swaps and sub-prime mortgages could ruin the world as we know it? So if no one told you about the last crisis, who do you think will alert you in advance of the next one?

Nearly half (48.6%) of chief financial officers in the U.S. believe this country will be in recession by the end of next year, according to the Duke University/CFO Global Business

33 "ALAN GREENSPAN: The bull market is over, and investors should 'run for cover'." https://markets.businessinsider.com/news/stocks/stock-market-news-alan-greenspan-warns-investors-to-run-for-cover-2018-12-1027818871. Rebecca Ungarino, 2018 2018. Web. 18 Dec 2018.

Outlook survey released on December 12, 2018. The Duke survey also found that 82% of CFOs believe that a recession will begin by the end of 2020.[34]

It seems like just a minute ago the US CFOs were embracing the mistaken notion that the US could enjoy 4% GDP growth. We've been saying for some time now what former Fed Reserve chair Janet Yellen said that, "quite high" levels of corporate debt are "a danger." Yellen is absolutely correct with her observation that, "High levels of corporate leverage could prolong the downturn and lead to lots of bankruptcies," she said on CNBC, December 10, 2018.[35]

**"It's tough to make predictions,
especially about the future."**

−Yogi Berra

---

34 "CFO Survey: Recession Likely by Year-End 2019." https://www.fuqua.duke.edu/duke-fuqua-insights/cfo-survey-december-2018. John Graham, 2018 2018. Web. 12 Dec 2018.
35 "Former Fed Chair Yellen says excessive corporate debt could prolong a downturn." https://www.cnbc.com/2018/12/11/janet-yellen-says-excessive-corporate-debt-could-prolong-a-downturn.html. Thomas Franck, CNBC 2018. Web. 10 Oct 2018..

According to me, it's not about the prediction, it's all about the preparation. We put far more emphasis on the work necessary to keep clients assets intact than attempting to predict what might happen or when it might happen.

I was asked to speak to 100 of my peers recently. I started by asking, how do you think that two story white house in Mexico Beach, Florida survived Hurricane Michael?

The first answer was, "It was God" and the second answer offered was, "It's a miracle." The third response was the correct answer, "They built it for the big one." The point I was making is that just as most houses are built in the same pattern, most portfolios are going to do the same thing at the same time. Like ordinary houses after a Category 4 hurricane, your assets could be devastated.

As we looked at a photo of one of the few houses left standing after Hurricane Michael I did everything I could to inspire my colleagues to approach the task as these home owners did. "It's the first house that either one of us had ever built," said Dr. Lebron Lackey, one of the homeowners. The house was built with concrete walls. The foundation included 40 foot pilings. Rebar is placed through all of the walls to increase stability. The additions added about 15%–20% more expense than usual.

In the investment world, cost is king. The lower the cost the better. But that answer addresses a different question. Now is the time for you to discover ways to 'run for cover' by keeping your assets intact begin by determining how much loss you can accept. Followed by how active management strategies can be applied on behalf of your personalized goals. Then look to see what asset classes outside of cash, bonds, stocks can be added to your portfolio. I count 8 asset classes at Yale Endowment, for example. A stool with eight legs is simply stronger than a two or three legged stool to hold up the weight. Even in a hurricane. And when it comes to cost, it is often the case that you get what you pay for.

Sometimes you have to pay more to keep more after a disaster.

"It's like déjà vu all over again."
– Yogi Berra

Suppose the CFOs are wrong about the severity and the timing. Just suppose it's not another recession around the corner, because it could turn out to be a worldwide Great Depression II. Something astrophysicist Michio Kaku, Ph.D. said at a 2014 conference I attended with my peers in 2018 should have happened ten years ago. Act as if another depression is in the cards. If it doesn't happen, who cares? If it does happen, prepared investors may be able to take advantage of opportunities they never saw coming. It's worth noting that on a per capita basis, more Americans became millionaires after the Great Depression than any other time in history. As I wrote just be before Thanksgiving: Be thankful for cash.

6

WHAT THE GOVERNMENT SHUTDOWN REVEALS ABOUT US

With the government shutdown in our rearview mirror, it's a good idea to identify the elephant in the room. Instead of saving at a level that can make work optional, retailers are delighted to see that Americans have embraced the mantra, 'Spend, baby, spend!" As I have stated on nationally syndicated TV and radio programs, our habit of spending is terrific for executive bonuses, stock prices, and company profits, but it does not work when the income stops and the spending continues.

The day after Christmas 2018 the DOW rocketed over 1,000 points, more than likely based on positive holiday sales data, as noted by Dent Research, December 28, 2018. The other side of that coin is that many shoppers purchased with credit as opposed to cash. Later the same day, the Richmond Fed reported a steep drop in its manufacturing index, while consumer confidence fell more than expected.[36]

My mother worked for the FAA as part of the team that reviewed pilot and air traffic controller medical records to keep flying safe. One of the things that I will always remember is how dedicated everyone I came to know was to doing their jobs. It is unfathomable to imagine thousands of federal government workers, and many contractors, who didn't get paid, leaving them embarrassed and suddenly close to homeless.

---

36 "What To Do With Your Investments in This Market." https://economyandmarkets.com/markets/investments-to-do-this-market/. Harry Dent, 2018 2018. Web. 28 Dec 2018.

I don't know how my original family would have fared, but I do know that in my home it was my mother who set aside money with each and every paycheck.

Today these government employees owe a total of $438 million per month in mortgage and rental payments, according to Zillow, which makes for an average of approximately $604 per month for each federal employee. Excluding benefits, the average federal salary is about $85,000 per year or about $7,000 per month submits former OMB Director, David Stockman. Stockman put things in perspective with this observation, "Indeed, the rot at America's economic foundation is almost completely invisible."[37]

In his message to subscribers on January 24, 2019, Stockman went on to say, "Half of U.S. households have no 'rainy day' funds. Fifty percent of tax filers earn under $40,000 per

37 "What the Government Shutdown Reveals About Us."
Corporate Counsel Men of Color. https://www.ccmenofcolor.org/
what-the-government-shutdown-reveals-about-us/. Marc Jeffrey.
2019. Web. 4 Feb 2019.

year. And even many of the labor aristocrats have no financial cushion. They live paycheck to paycheck on monthly dispensations from Uncles Sam, as the case may be.[38]

How in the world can the U.S. economy be described as 'strong?' Yet the minutes from the last seven meetings of the Federal Open Market Committee show that 'strong,' 'stronger,' and 'strongly' were used between 24 and 32 times per meeting."

"It is everywhere a problem of delusion and debt."

— David Stockman

As of January 24, 2019, the U.S. net debt outstanding stands at \$21.957 trillion. Which is up from \$20.679 trillion just one year ago. Stockman said, "There's no 'supply side miracle' happening, as federal tax receipts are plunging despite that Trump 'stimulus.'" Now before we

38 "What the Government Shutdown Reveals About Us."
Corporate Counsel Men of Color. https://www.ccmenofcolor.org/what-the-government-shutdown-reveals-about-us/. Marc Jeffrey. 2019. Web. 4 Feb 2019.

start pointing fingers at our leaders let's take a look at household debt. Stockman asserts, "Household debt now stands at $15.6 trillion. It's actually up by $1.4 trillion from the fourth quarter of 2007."[39]

So we are all in this together, and no one gets a pass. If you don't save for yourself, who is going to do it for you? It's a new year. And it's time for a different approach. "For the last quarter century, the American personal savings rate has usually been below 10 percent, and often below 5 percent. In the aggregate, most Americans simply don't save enough. This is quite aside from any misfortune they might encounter or hardship they might have inflicted on them — and federal employees certainly suffered from both," wrote Tyler Cowen at Bloomberg, January 28, 2019.[40]

39 "What the Government Shutdown Reveals About Us." Corporate Counsel Men of Color. https://www.ccmenofcolor.org/what-the-government-shutdown-reveals-about-us/. Marc Jeffrey. 2019. Web. 4 Feb 2019.
40 "One Shutdown Lesson Is That Americans Need to Save More." https://www.bloomberg.com/opinion/articles/2019-01-28/shutdown-lesson-americans-need-to-save-more. Tyler Cowen, Bloomberg Opinion 2019. Web. 2 Feb 2019.

If you lost your income for a month or two you would make adjustments. Rather than wait for something like that to happen to you out of the blue, get to the point where you spend 80% of what you earn and save 20% for tomorrow. Bloomberg observed, "Indeed a higher savings rate is possible, and not just for the wealthy. Most Mormons in the U.S., for example, manage to tithe at least 10 percent of their incomes. This suggests it is possible to curtail one's consumption without losing the best things in life. Mormons also tend to have especially large families, making tithing all the more difficult. If Mormons can tithe so much, is it so impossible for the rest of us, including government employees, to save more?"[41]

In the same article we read, "In China, where per-capita income is closer to that of Mexico than the U.S., household savings rates are often well over 30 percent. One reason for this may be

41 "One Shutdown Lesson Is That Americans Need to Save More." https://www.bloomberg.com/opinion/articles/2019-01-28/ shutdown-lesson-americans-need-to-save-more. Tyler Cowen, Bloomberg Opinion 2019. Web. 2 Feb 2019.

that the Chinese know their economic futures might be extremely volatile, and thus they hold funds in reserve."[42]

Complacency is a luxury Americans cannot afford. Start with your very next paycheck by setting aside 5 percent of your gross income. Notice how you don't feel any pain at all. But even if the savings level becomes painful you know you are preparing for the unforeseen in 2019 and beyond.

---

42 "One Shutdown Lesson Is That Americans Need to Save More." https://www.bloomberg.com/opinion/articles/2019-01-28/ shutdown-lesson-americans-need-to-save-more, Tyler Cowen, Bloomberg Opinion 2019. Web. 2 Feb 2019.

Our Financial & Insurance Calculators. Please use your smartphone QR code scanner to be easily directed there.

Scan here:

7

Three Ways Investors Can Prepare For a Future No One Can Predict

As you may know, I have a real problem with those in my industry who tell investors to literally 'do nothing' as they watch their life savings disappear into thin air. No matter where we are in the world or where our money might be at a given time it makes a great deal of sense to prepare in advance your exit strategy in the event of real and present danger. This is not a recommendation, but it is an easy example from which every investor can learn. It's a 1-2 punch to keep you from getting your assets handed to you.

In the following example, Greater Diversification produced less declines and higher account balance.

Slide 1. Notice how a traditional buy and hold in stocks did well and how an investor who owned two additional asset classes did better. The decline wasn't as severe in 2000–02 and 2008–09. If your account held up better than most the last two times in the same decade markets were off 50% your portfolio may hold up better the next time the grits hit the pan.

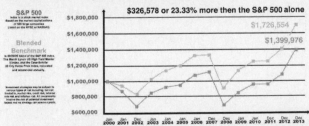

Source: Yale Endowment, Investor's Advantage Corp.

For full regulatory disclosures, please see my website www.whybepoor.com. Diversification seeks to reduce the volatility of a portfolio by investing in a variety of asset classes. Neither asset allocation nor diversification guarantee against market loss or greater or more consistent returns. An investor cannot invest directly in an index. All examples are hypothetical.

Limiting losses can maintain your cash flow

Slide 2. In the second scenario we show what happened when the investor needed to withdraw $60,000 a year from their retirement balance of $1,000,000 the beginning of 2001. In both cases over $600,000 was withdrawn, but the portfolio with three asset classes held up better than the investor with only one type of investment vehicle. We can agree that three legs supporting your life savings is better than one.

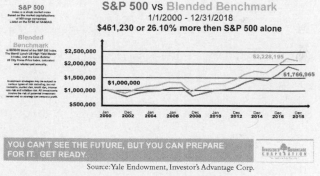

Source: Yale Endowment, Investor's Advantage Corp.

For full regulatory disclosures, please see my website www. whybepoor.com. Diversification seeks to reduce the volatility of a portfolio by investing in a variety of asset classes. Neither asset allocation nor diversification guarantee against market loss or greater or more consistent returns. An investor cannot invest directly in an index. All examples are hypothetical.

Active Management systems can work like a thermostat to determine daily, is the call risk off or risk on?

Slide 3. As the Recession Monitor shown in red went north and stocks in blue went south, shares of stocks were sold to reduce losses. 2008 started with 5% of the portfolio in cash or money markets, shown in green, but you can see at the black arrow client money market accounts expanded to 60% of their account. Think risk off in 2008 as the markets had every investor running for cover. Think risk on in 2009 when negative volatility turned positive. Over time you can see that the percentage of cash moved back to 5% when the market gained its footing. Investors deserve to employ teams that look at their accounts daily to determine is it time to pour more fuel on the fire in an upmarket or water on the fire during severe downturns.

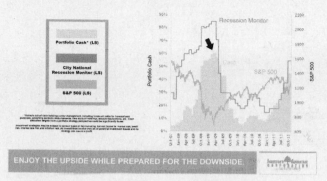

Source: Yale Endowment, Investor's Advantage Corp.

For full regulatory disclosures, please see my website www.whybepoor.com. Diversification seeks to reduce the volatility of a portfolio by investing in a variety of asset classes. Neither asset allocation nor diversification guarantee against market loss or greater or more consistent returns. An investor cannot invest directly in an index. All examples are hypothetical.

Neither Active Management Nor Diversification guarantee against market loss or greater or more consistent returns.

8

WITH CONSUMER CONFIDENCE THE HIGHEST SINCE 2000, WHAT'S NEXT?

Based on data collected through February 15, the most recent Conference Board Consumer Confidence Index was released on February 27, 2018. "Consumer confidence improved to its highest level since 2000 (Nov. 2000, 132.6) after a modest increase in January," said Lynn Franco, Director of Economic Indicators at The Conference Board. Franco went on to say, "Consumers' assessment of current conditions was more favorable this month, with the labor force the main driver. Despite the recent stock market volatility, consumers expressed greater optimism about short-term prospects for business and labor market conditions, as well as their financial prospects. Overall, consumers remain quite confident that the economy will continue expanding at a strong pace in the months ahead." I asked my 10-year-old grand-niece who is fond of math to study this chart and tell me what she thought was next. She said, "It looks like it could be danger ahead to me." I agree.[43]

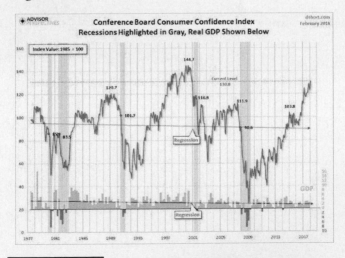

43 "The Conference Board Consumer Confidence Index Declined in March." Market Watch. https://www.marketwatch.com/press-release/the-conference-board-consumer-confidence-index-declined-in-march-2019-03-26. 2019. Web. 26 March 2019.

We know we shouldn't judge a book by its cover, but we do. We know we should study the data for a while before jumping to conclusions, but we are too busy gushing over the 'good news.' When consumer confidence is high many investors agree that the stock market melt up is in full swing. However, Mark Hulbert at MarketWatch on March 20, 2018 opines, "I found that consumer confidence is a meaningful contrarian indicator in the stock market. Like other sentiment indicators, consumer confidence tends to rise and fall along with the stock market itself.[44]

Accordingly, consumers are most confident at market tops (bold added), just as they are most pessimistic at market bottoms." Hulbert asserts what many consider to be a bullish indicator is actually a market warning sign. In fact, he suggests, "It's time to lighten up on stocks and build up cash." That may be a perfect thing

44 "Opinion: This bullish economic news is a warning for the stock market." https://www.marketwatch.com/story/this-bullish-economic-news-is-a-warning-for-the-stock-market-2018-03-20. Mark Hulbert, MarketWatch 2018. Web. 20 March 2018.

to add to the list of things to do for the do-it-yourself investor. For those who realize they are too busy to sell in some random fashion, let alone know when in advance to get back in, now is the time to investigate active management strategies. Since, according to me, it's not about the prediction, it's all about the preparation, ask your financial advisor to show you or kick the tires at the investment management firms that have shown capability with moving out of risk assets to cash instruments in a bad year and purposefully moved back into risk assets, like bond and or stock accounts in a good year. Savvy investors are like tennis players, you have to play both sides of the net. Investors hate losses more than they like gains. Harry Dent, Dent Research charts two possibilities. The bearish scenario is that a market top was made on January 26. The bullish outcome may be a result of a DOW top around 28,000.[45]

45 "Opinion: This bullish economic news is a warning for the stock market." https://www.marketwatch.com/story/this-bullish-economic-news-is-a-warning-for-the-stock-market-2018-03-20. Mark Hulbert, Market Watch 2018. Web. 20 March 2018.

"The markets have been very tricky in this final orgasmic bubble, especially since the Trump win in early November 2016. Unless the market quickly reverses and breaks through the upper trend-line of this 'Pennant Pattern', then the direction is very likely down," said Harry Dent on March 19, 2018. It's impossible to see the future. So let's speak hypothetically about the ridiculous. I mean, who told you in 2007 that something you never heard of before, like credit default swaps could possibly end life as you know it on this planet. It is also worth noting the Nasdaq -80% loss in the 2000–02 tech wreck that took 15 long years to fully recover, submits Adam Shell, USA TODAY, April 23, 2015. It's all about the preparation. Look to see if the DOW breaks to the upside above 24,000 or breaks below that level. It may be that the DOW rallies to 29,000 this year. From either level, it may be that an initial crash of about -40% occurs. Then we may wonder, how low could it go? Is it possible you can address the problem before it happens? You know consumer confidence will drop.[46]

What is in your control is assessing how much risk you are willing to take. In fact, you can determine now how much loss you are willing to accept. When disaster strikes there is no time to plan. And after the grits hit the pan there may not be enough time to recover. So take the time now to see what you can do to limit your losses. You are going to need all of the money.

Neither Active Management Nor Diversification guarantee against market loss or greater or more consistent returns.

---

46 "Could Gold's Day in the Sun Be Upon Us?." https://economyandmarkets.com/economy/golds-day-in-the-sun-coming-soon/. Harry Dent, Economy & Markets 2018. Web. 14 Feb 2018.

9

Two Reasons Why Healthcare Costs Keep Rising

Let me address the elephant in the room before I tackle the healthcare issues. The current market volatility is due in large part to burgeoning signs of an all-out trade war. On March 9, 2018, in an effort to restore an American industry to its previous luster, President Trump garishly imposed a 25% tariff on steel imports and a 10% tariff on aluminum imports. With the tariffs taking effect on March 24 only Canada, Mexico, and South Korea are exempt.

A tariff is a duty or tax placed on certain goods by the government. The design is to make foreign goods costlier giving an advantage to domestic manufacturers of the same products who don't have to pay the tax.

The tariffs may be a shot in the arm for steel and aluminum companies in the U.S.A, but in the event of increased demand here it may not be that American manufacturers have the capacity to meet a gigantic swell. There are a couple of things that give my friend, Charles Sizemore, CFA, Dent Research and me pause. First, when either of us hears talk of "winning a trade war," it is our opinion that there are no winners in a trade war. Just losers, as the tax is ultimately passed on to the consumer. It is not unusual for President Trump to make blustering pronouncements one day followed by complete silence the next. In the meantime, do not be surprised to see China use Trump's new tariffs to its advantage. Markets are not fond of uncertainty.

My second very real concern is suppose the noise of a trade war becomes real news. Sizemore puts it in historical perspective. "The

Great Depression didn't start out as 'great'. It was a deep but not necessarily extraordinary recession. That is, until Senator Reed Smoot and Representative Will Hawley pushed through the Smoot-Hawley Tariff in 1930, one of the highest and broadest tariffs in U.S. history." Of course, the intent should sound very familiar, in this case, to breathe new life into the American farming industry that has been struggling for some time. We are not in a trade war yet. So far we are seeing a war of words. But if the tit-for-tat escalates, all bets are off. It's 'a terrifically bad idea,' according to The Economist, March 8, 2018.

Sizemore says he does not "expect a repeat of the 1930's here." I say, it's not about the prediction, it's all about the preparation. If no one saw the Great Depression coming down the pike, who do you expect you can count on to be your canary in the coal mine in the event Great Depression II is baked into the cake? Please do recognize the DOW lost -89% in 24 months from 1929–32 according to Yahoo Finance.

That means what was $1M in 1929 became about $108k in 1932. What's more, assuming investors did not sell or spend any money, it took about 20 years for the account to fully recover. Do also keep in mind, if you were born in 1900 your life expectancy was about 57 years. Which means you may not have had the luxury of time to get back to even before death. Regret is like guilt. They are two gifts that keep on giving.

I believe success leaves clues. Billionaire Mark Cuban said on the one hand he sees stock market swings as a buying opportunity. On the other hand, he said he "decided to hedge" his moves after seeing investors get wiped out, on CNBC, February 13, 2018. Cuban is a busy man with a net worth of $3.7B, according to Forbes, April 3, 2018. **But, if Cuban isn't too preoccupied with life to put his hedging strategies in place on his life savings before the grits hit**

the pan, you and I can make keeping our assets intact the priority it deserves too.[47]

The first reason health care costs keep rising is because we are all getting older. In fact, 10,000 people a day are turning 65 through the mid-2030's, submits Jeff Hanson, CEO, Griffin-American Healthcare. I asked Harry Dent, Dent Research for his take. Dent said, April 2, 2018, "A reason our healthcare costs about twice as much as it does in other developed countries is because our system is full of B.S. special interests and insurance bureaucracy that adds layers and layers of costs. Every step of this chain of special interests is locked in by decades of lobbying efforts." Dent went on to say, "There's no market with less rationality and greater cost disincentives than our very own U.S. healthcare system."

Dent opined our "perverted, special-interest driven system needs to break down and be re-

47 "Mark Cuban: 'There was blood in the street' — here's the way I'm hedging the market swings." https://www.cnbc.com/2018/02/13/here-is-the-way-mark-cuban-hedged-the-market-meltdown.html. Matthew J. Belvedere, https://www.cnbc.com/2018/02/13/here-is-the-way-mark-cuban-hedged-the-market-meltdown.html 2018. Web. 13 Feb 2018.

created from the bottom up." The job could be done with a "consumer–driven, direct primary care systems that make both doctors and consumers accountable for real service," asserts Dent. Design health insurance to take care of the more extreme situations so there would not be arcane bureaucracy to the system. Such an arrangement would put an end to the endless incentives to go for the "all you can test buffet," Dent said.

"More American millionaires were created during the Great Depression than in any other period," declared Jonathan Jones at evancarmichael.com. To the extent you keep your assets intact you can take advantage of opportunities that are probably impossible to foresee. A serious downturn may be the perfect time for the health care industry to go through a revolution. The beginning of a new nation in 1776 wasn't fun, but it changed everything. Change is good.[48]

48 Evanmichael.com. 2018. Web. 3 April 2018

Our Financial & Insurance Calculators. Please use your smartphone QR code scanner to be easily directed there.

Scan here:

10

A TARIFFICALLY BAD IDEA

The market volatility is due in large part to burgeoning signs of an all-out trade war. On March 9, 2018, in an effort to restore an American industry to its previous luster, President Trump garishly imposed a 25% tariff on steel imports and a 10% tariff on aluminum imports. Mid-June this year, in addition to pledging further investment restrictions, the Trump administration announced tariffs on $50 billion in Chinese imports.

Beijing responded quickly escalating the dispute. China intends to impose tariffs with "equal scale, equal intensity" on imports from the U.S., and all of the country's earlier trade commitments are now off the table, the Commerce Ministry said in a statement on its website late June 15, according to Yahoo Finance. Let me explain; A tariff is a duty or tax placed on particular goods by the government. The design is to make foreign goods more costly, giving an advantage to domestic manufacturers of the same products who don't have to pay the tax. The tariffs may be a shot in the arm for steel and aluminum companies in the U.S.A, but in the event of increased demand here, it may not be that American manufacturers have the capacity to meet a gigantic swell. There are a couple of things that give my friend, Charles Sizemore, CFA, Dent Research and me pause. First, when we hear talk of "winning a trade war," it is our opinion that there are no winners in that war. Just losers, as the tax is ultimately passed on to the consumer. It is not unusual for President

Trump to make blustering pronouncements one day followed by complete silence the next.[49]

In the meantime, do not be surprised to see China use Trump's new tariffs to its advantage. You know markets are not fond of uncertainty. You won't be surprised to watch Wall Street move lower on President Trump 's rising trade tensions. No one knows how things may turn out, but we can see how such moves have turned out in our history. "It's like deja-vu all over again!" – Yogi Berra My second genuine concern, suppose the noise of a trade war becomes real news. Sizemore puts it in historical perspective. "The Great Depression didn't start out as 'great'. It was a deep but not necessarily extraordinary recession.

That is until Senator Reed Smoot and Representative Will Hawley pushed through the Smoot-Hawley Tariff in 1930, one of the highest and broadest tariffs in U.S. history." Of

---

49 "What you need to know on Wall Street today." https://finance. yahoo.com/news/know-wall-street-today-161755896.html. Olivia Oran, Yahoo Finance 2018. Web. 5 Jun 2018.

course, the intent should sound very familiar, in this case, to breathe new life into the American farming industry that has been struggling for some time. We are not in a trade war yet. So far we've seen a war of words. But if the tit-for-tat escalates, all bets are off. It's 'a tariffically bad idea,' according to The Economist, March 8, 2018. What we can learn Sizemore says he does not "expect a repeat of the 1930's here." I say, it's not about the prediction, it's all about the preparation. If no one saw the Great Depression coming down the pike, who do you expect you can count on to be your canary in the coal mine in the event Great Depression II is baked into the cake?

Please do recognize the DOW lost -89% in 24 months from 1929-32 according to Yahoo Finance. That means what was $1M in 1929 became about $108k in 1932. What's more, assuming investors did not sell or spend any money, it took about 20 years for the account to recover fully. Do also keep in mind, if you were born 1900 your life expectancy was about 57 years, which means you may not have had the luxury of time to get back to even before death. Regret is like guilt. They are two gifts that keep on giving. Be like Cuban, hedge baby, hedge I believe success leaves clues. Billionaire Mark Cuban said, on the one hand, he sees stock market swings as a buying opportunity. On the other hand, he said he "decided to hedge" his moves after seeing investors get wiped out, on CNBC, February 13, 2018.[50]

Cuban is a busy man with a net worth of $3.7B, according to Forbes, April 3, 2018. But, if Cuban isn't too preoccupied with life to put his hedging strategies in place on his life savings before the grits hit the pan, you and I can make keeping our assets intact the priority it deserves too. Some really good news "More American millionaires were created during the Great Depression than in any other period," declared

50 "History of bear markets since 1929." https://finance.yahoo.com/news/history-bear-markets-since-1929-143729786.html. . Jade Scipioni, Yahoo Finance 2018. Web. 26 Dec 2018.

Jonathan Jones at evancarmichael.com. To the extent you keep your assets intact, you can take advantage of opportunities that are probably impossible to foresee. A severe downturn may not be much different than a frigid winter. Some creatures and plants slow down and die in the winter. At the same time, severe cold brings dramatic change which helps others get stronger and survive. While winter can get uncomfortable, only the strong survive. Therefore, if you've prepared, change is good.[51]

---

51 Evanmichael.com. 2018. Web. 3 April 2018

11

OUR 'ECONOMIC PONZI SCHEME' MAY CAUSE THE NEXT CRASH

Despite 39 years in the securities business it always catches me by surprise when investors proclaim they do not have the stomach to even use the words 'market loss.' Now I come from a fine family of Polly Anna's but I have learned to look both ways more than once when crossing the street. That's every street, every time, no exceptions. What makes the conversation even more interesting is when we get to the math on money in the bank.

Some investors have gotten so risk averse they have a very hard time recognizing that money in the bank only preserves principal. But that's all it is doing for you. As the banks make money on your money, after inflation and income taxes on your earnings you are accepting a guaranteed loss every year and you will not make it up with volume. So let's keep it real. Do you prefer a guaranteed loss or a possible loss? Some investors are taking advantage of new technology that allows you to quantify your threshold for loss.

This work is followed by developing a customized portfolio that may perform within your win/loss parameters. Investors can even review portfolio performance over the past ten years. This is meaningful as it valuable to see, unlike most investors, how bad the losses were and how long it took for your account to fully recover. When you can see how you might have weathered the last storm it does afford you some confidence that you may be better prepared for the next hurricane. Rather than blindly repeat the past, let's see what we can learn to be better prepared for the good, the bad, and the unforeseen. Former economics professor, now president of Hussman Investment Trust, John Hussman claims the economic system today is "dysfunctional." Hussman has become known as a 'perma-bear' partially due to his forecast of a market decline exceeding 60% as well as a full decade of negative returns. Only time will tell, but he says the economy is setting the market up for unprecedented failure, according to Business Insider, June 11, 2018. [52]

If there is any combination of withdrawal and market loss that produces a 60% drawdown, you need a gain of 150% to get back to even. In sharp contrast, if the drawdown is 20% the gain needs to be 25% to get back to your starting value. I am encouraging you to place your bets where you can see the loss might be limited. This way you can stay in the game as opposed to run of money before you run out of time. As we have discussed previously, good strategy preparation is particularly important when

---

52 *Business Insider*. 2018. Web 11 June 2018

income must be taken from retirement accounts. After age 72 you cannot stop taking income and in fact, such income from traditional retirement accounts must increase every year for the rest of your life.

Your account recovered thanks to a strong market and contributions when you were working. After sustaining a 60% loss, what was $1m becomes $400,000.Take another withdrawal and your chances of complete recovery may well be zero. Hussman and I agree that the biggest hurdle today is how consumers, companies, and governments are more indebted than any other time in history. Excessive debt can lead to major defaults and investor angst. Hussman explained in a recent blog post, "The hallmark of an economic Ponzi scheme is that the operation of the economy relies on the constant creation of low-grade debt in order to finance consumption and income shortfalls among some members of the economy, using the massive surpluses earned by other members of the economy,". "The debt burdens, speculation, and skewed valuations most responsible for today's lopsided prosperity are exactly the seeds from which the next crisis will spring."[53]

Harry Dent, Dent Research asserts the politicians and central bankers are doing everything in their power to keep the artificial bubble in the air. I sure hope Harry is an accurate forecaster when he opines, "These politicians will be roasted in history, not just for creating the greatest bubble ever, but for extending it far beyond any logic." Before the last election Harry did say no matter who becomes president, the musical chairs will stop between 2017 and 2020. He went on to say whoever takes office will not be re-elected. Now the Republicans will likely lose the House, perhaps the Senate, and there hasn't been a crash or downturn yet.'

That tax cut that favored business profits, along with the top 1% to 10% who tend to

53 "Hallmark of an Economic Ponzi Scheme." https://www. hussmanfunds.com/comment/mc180604/. . John P. Hussman, Ph.D., Hussman Funds 2018. Web. 12 June 2018.

own them, is not working so well. So let's have another one![54]

In this nine-year bull market companies don't need tax cuts, let alone more. Harry explains the primary reason, "Wages and salaries, as a percent of GDP, peaked in 1970 at 51.7% and fell dramatically to 42.1% in late 2011. They're currently around 43%. That's a fall of 29%. From 1945 to 1974 wages in the last great boom and bust average about 50% of GDP. They were more stable and hence no extremes in income inequality or stock crashes greater than 20% happened during the Bob Hope boom from 1942 to 1968."[55]

When I actually paid attention in my high school history class on World War II I will always remember the statement, 'A convoy has

54 "Corporate Profits Are Crushing Wages, And The Tax Cuts Aren't Helping." https://talkmarkets.com/content/economics--politics/corporate-profits-are-crushing-wages-and-the-tax-cuts-arent-helping?post=179292. Harry Dent, Talk Markets 2018. Web. 12 Jun 2018.
55 "Corporate Profits Are Crushing Wages, And The Tax Cuts Aren't Helping." https://talkmarkets.com/content/economics--politics/corporate-profits-are-crushing-wages-and-the-tax-cuts-arent-helping?post=179292. Harry Dent, Talk Markets 2018. Web. 12 Jun 2018.

to travel at the speed of the slowest vessel.' The top 1% to 10% have enjoyed a majority of the wage and wealth gains in past decades. Mergers and acquisitions don't do much for every day Americans. Look out below. Hussman's expected market losses may turn out to be conservative.

"Neither Active Management Nor Diversification guarantee against market loss or greater or more consistent returns."

12

IT'S EASIER TO LOSE MONEY THAN TO MAKE MONEY

The stock market has been responding positively to better than expected earnings, "The Melt Up is officially here. This is the boom we've been waiting for. And this phase should last 12 to 18 months", said Steve Sjuggerud, Stansberry Research. He went on to say, "The Melt Up will propel U.S. stocks to fantastic heights. The Melt Up is the final push of a bull market. It's when the leading companies of this near decade-long boom really take off and propel the overall market dramatically higher."[56]

As I have written before, do not be complacent, you must be vigilant. Please enjoy the melt-up as you prepare for a melt-down. I don't know what the catalyst might be for a reversal of fortune, but we all see the huge elephant in the room. Charles Sizemore, CFA, Dent Research put a trade war in historical perspective. "The Great Depression didn't start out as 'great'. It was a deep but not necessarily extraordinary recession. That is until Senator Reed Smoot and Representative Will Hawley pushed through the Smoot-Hawley Tariff in 1930, one of the highest and broadest tariffs in U.S. history." Of course, the intent should sound very familiar, in this case, by imposing a 40% tariff on 20,000 goods, to breathe new life into the American farming industry that has been struggling for some time. We are not in a trade war yet. So far we've seen

56 "The 'Melt Up' Is Officially Underway." https://
stansberryresearch.com/articles/the-melt-up-is-officially-
underway-3. Steve Sjuggerud, Stansberry Research 2018. Web. 31
July 2018.

a war of words. But as the tit-for-tat escalates, all bets are off. It's 'a tariffically bad idea,' according to The Economist, March 8, 2018.[57]

As a child, I was always amazed to hear about the families enjoying the fireworks on their street celebrating the Fourth of July who noticed after all of the excitement that somehow someone accidentally put their own house on fire. Playing with fire is fun until the result becomes a catastrophe. Unintended consequences are my real concern with a trade war.

No matter what the market may do, Linda Ferentchak, Proactive Advisor Magazine, put forth two very realistic scenarios. She points out that for those with a 2005 starting balance of $500,000 in the S&P 500 who didn't take any withdrawals, the account would be worth about $1.1 million by year end 2017. But if it were the case that you retired that year by setting up withdrawals of 6% a year or $2,640 per month,

57 "The Difference Between Good Inflation and Bad Inflation." https://charlessizemore.tumblr.com/post/172040106091/the-difference-between-good-inflation-and-bad. Charles Sizemore, Charles Sizemore's Tumblr 2018. Web. 19 March 2018.

by 2017, your year-end value would be less than $355,000. Withdrawals total $406,560, "but another bear market could easily result in the account running out of money." Ferentchak goes on to say, "While the long-term trend of the market has historically been to the upside, it is very difficult for a retiree to recover from a market decline if the individual also needs to be making withdrawals from the portfolio to meet living expenses.[58]

The drag from withdrawing funds from a retirement portfolio can quickly turn a market downturn into retirement shortfall. It's all a matter of math. If your portfolio declines by 40%, it takes a 67% gain to return to its prior high. Add in the drag of steady withdrawals and recovering becomes even more difficult." If not, impossible. The combination of one severe market loss and annual withdrawals can quickly

---

58 "Active management: Don't retire without it." http://proactiveadvisormagazine.com/active-management-dont-retire-without-it/. Linda Ferentchak, Proactive Advisor Magazine 2018. Web. 18 July 2018.

reveal that investors could well run out of money before they run out of time.

The difference is the result of changing the investor's portfolio from passive management to active management. Instead of holding risk assets, most notably during 2008, actively managed accounts went from shares to cash, then back into risk assets in 2009 as the market enjoyed volatility to the upside.

While passive accounts may have taken nearly four years to get back to even, actively managed accounts may have taken less than two years. Active investment strategies can be applied to bond and fixed-income portfolios as well as to help reduce market losses. Once the funds are gone for whatever reason, be it market losses or withdrawals or some combination of the two, it doesn't matter how quickly the market recovers.

If a downdraft combination becomes minus 60%, the investor needs a gain of 150% to get back to even. Now we're talking a hail-Mary pass just to get back in the game. Clearly, such odds are a long shot at best. When an investor can keep losses and withdrawals to 20%, the math is a gain of 25% is needed to get back to the starting value. Those are losses from which you may recover. At least the odds are more in your favor. "Active management: Don't retire without it," wrote Ferentchak, July 18, 2018.[59]

Neither Active Management Nor Diversification guarantee against market loss or greater or more consistent returns.

---

59 "Active management: Don't retire without it." http://proactiveadvisormagazine.com/active-management-dont-retire-without-it/. Linda Ferentchak, Proactive Advisor Magazine 2018. Web. 18 July 2018.

13

How Trade Tariffs Could Crush California's $2.7 Trillion Economy

As we learned with the 1930 Smoot-Hawley Act, tariffs can backfire on the country that believes it's a relatively painless way to affect change. By applying 40% tariffs on 20,000 incoming goods to the U.S. to protect our farmers, it may be the singular event that caused America to move past a serious recession to The Great Depression. Unintended consequences is what can happen when one plays with fire. Sometimes you end up burning down your own house.

The latest federal data show China's response to raise tariffs on many American goods will have a significant impact on California's economy. China is one of the largest recipients of California exports. Last year, California exported about $16.3 billion in goods to mainland China, according to the U.S. Census Bureau. Another $9.9 billion in exports went to Hong Kong, a free port that is part of China. U.S. law treats Hong Kong as a separate jurisdiction from China. Exports to greater China (China & Hong Kong) last year were equivalent to almost 1% of California's gross domestic product. (Source: The Sacramento Bee, May 14, 2019.[60]

---

60 "Trade war with China could hit California hard. Here's how.." https://www.sacbee.com/news/politics-government/article230342089.html. Phillip Reese, The Sacramento Bee 2019. Web. 14 May 2019.

California ranks #5 in global GDP outranking the U.K. last year, says USA Today, May 5, 2018. California sent more exports to greater China last year than to any other country except Mexico. It sent more exports to mainland China than any other countries, except Canada and Mexico. The value of California exports to greater China has grown by about $8 billion, or more than 40% in the last decade after adjusting for inflation. The value of exports to mainland China has grown by about $5 billion, also more than 40%. Five sectors comprise about 70% of California's exports to both mainland and greater China. Computer and electronics products, machinery, transportation equipment, chemicals and scrap and waste, according to the Sacramento Bee.[61]

---

61 "Trade war with China could hit California hard. Here's how.." https://www.sacbee.com/news/politics-government/article230342089.html. Phillip Reese, The Sacramento Bee 2019. Web. 14 May 2019.

Here are the truths that have nothing to do with politics. The overarching message from the U.S. business community must be: When the U.S. engages openly in free and fair trade, we all win. Competition makes the country better, encouraging industry around the world to deliver more value to more people. Trade is not zero sum. It helps to grow the standards of living of people around the globe. We need the inexpensive products from outside the country to raise our standard of living. And, with only 5 percent of the world population, we need open access to markets for our own goods to grow our economy. We cannot have one without the other.

But overall, free trade is beneficial to the U.S. Because of free trade, Americans enjoy higher living standards and a wider variety of more affordable products like clothing and electronics. Imports from low-cost countries deliver products at lower prices to consumers.

Imports actually boost the purchasing power of the average American household by approximately $18,000, according to the Peterson Institute for International Economics. These products sell because American consumers choose to buy them, and they are more affordable because they are made in low-cost regions. Mom is right about unintended consequences. Don't play with sharp saws or start a fire.[62]

---

62 "Big-screen TVs and other products you buy that may get more expensive because of a possible trade war with China." https://www.cnbc.com/2018/04/04/big-screen-tvs-and-other-products-you-buy-that-may-get-more-expensive-because-of-a-possible-trade-war-with-china.html. Evelyn Cheng, CNBC 2019. Web. 14 May 2019.

14

ARE WE BRACING FOR 2020 RECESSION?

According to me, it's not about the prediction. It's all about the preparation. On June 12, 2019, the predictions are suddenly coming in hard and heavy. The headlines read, "America's CFOs are bracing for a 2020 recession." Nearly half (48.1%) of chief financial officers in the United States are predicting the American economy will be in recession by the middle of next year, according to the Duke University/CFO Global Business Outlook survey released on Wednesday. And 69% of those executives are bracing for a recession by the end of 2020, according to Yahoo Finance, June 12, 2019[63]

"Next global financial crisis will strike in 2020, sparked by automated trading systems," warns JPMorgan, The Independent.[64]

"2020s Might Be The Worst Decade In U.S. History, triggered by contagion from a global credit crisis," says Forbes.[65]

"2020 is a real inflection point," asserts Mark Zandi, chief economist, Moody's Analytics.[66]

While no one can see the future, here's what we do know. Global stimulus packages are coming to an end. Inflation is rearing its head, and the trade disputes create as much greater

---

63 "Are we heading into a recession? Some CFOs think it could happen soon." https://finance.yahoo.com/news/heading-recession-cfos-think-could-100518329.html. Megan Henney, CNBC 2019. Web. 12 June 2019.
64 "Next global financial crisis will strike in 2020, warns investment bank JPMorgan." https://www.independent.co.uk/news/business/news/next-financial-crisis-2020-recession-world-markets-jpmorgan-a8540341.html. Peter Stubley, Independent 2018. Web. 12 June 2019.
65 "The 2020s Might Be The Worst Decade In U.S. History." https://www.forbes.com/sites/johnmauldin/2018/05/24/the-2020s-might-be-the-worst-decade-in-u-s-history/#4600566d48d3. John Mauldin, Forbes 2018. Web. 12 June 2019.
66 "The 2020s Might Be The Worst Decade In U.S. History." https://www.forbes.com/sites/johnmauldin/2018/05/24/the-2020s-might-be-the-worst-decade-in-u-s-history/#4600566d48d3. John Mauldin, Forbes 2018. Web. 12 June 2019.

uncertainty as they create a drag on economies at the same time interest rates are likely to continue upward. The 'immigration crisis' will slow growth at the same time aging populations are incapable of taking up the slack. This irony will likely be lost by the same demographic that voted for populist movements to remove them.

So, I am not predicting a recession in 2020. In fact, most economists forecast a recession only after it has started. Economists are masters of hindsight, but perhaps closer to apprentices at foresight.

"It was pure vainglory that drove the President of the United States of America to call into CNBC's 'Squawk Box.' Last Friday, he tweeted, 'Dow Jones has best week of the year!' His re-election rides on the stock market. When the recession happens, the proximate cause will be new tariffs and the Trade War. The inevitable downturn will really be about easy money – too much of it for too long," opined former OMB

Director, David Stockman, in his June 11, 2019 message to subscribers.[67]

Stockman went on to say, "It won't matter that the collapse of this Everything Bubble is decades in the making. The Great Disruptor will be guilty. We're already on the slippery slope. The incoming data are uniformly bad, except for ultra-lagging indicators like initial claims for state unemployment benefits and consumer confidence"[68]

Rather than attempt to predict the future it makes more sense to me to learn from history. When we don't learn from history it is reasonable to this observer that we will roughly repeat it. The two highlights about the Great Depression include stocks off -89% while New York real estate was off 60%. While stocks took 20 years to recover, NYC real estate took four decades to get back to its high water mark. Both

67 "Stockman: Economy Will Plunge Into a Recession Due to Trade War Escalation and Easy Money Policies." Dir. . Perf. David Stockman . CNBC, 2019. Video.
68 "Stockman: Economy Will Plunge Into a Recession Due to Trade War Escalation and Easy Money Policies." Dir. . Perf. David Stockman . CNBC, 2019. Video.

events took place in about 24 months. When this information is shared with investors they are hard pressed to comprehend exactly what happened. Which means, investors have even more imagining how the emotions will run amok should something like this happen again. If you are, however, prepared for the worst case scenario you are more likely to weather the storm. Unless you think you think like way too many category 4 hurricane victims who washed away in the belief they could "ride this one out."

Desperate times call for common sense measures. To avoid future shock and awe, answer these questions while you can.

1) How much risk can you accept?
2) How did your portfolio hold up 4th quarter 2018 and 2008?
3) What can you see to minimize losses?
4) What active management strategies can you identify that moved out of risk

assets to cash in 2008 and back into risk assets from safety in 2009?

5) What investments can you add like legs to your portfolio stool?

It's rarely the bus you see that can disrupt your day when crossing the street. The bus of disruption is typically one you did not see, you could not time, and there was no chance to get the license plates. So let's be ridiculous and say Depression II is baked into the cake well ahead of predictions to begin this year, not 2020. Now is the time to prepare for the good, the bad, and the unforeseen in 2019.

Neither Active Management Nor Diversification guarantee against market loss or greater or more consistent returns.

15

WHAT'S DRIVING THIS MARKET? IT'S NOT INVESTORS.

Larry Kudlow recently suggested there'd be no more interest-rate increases by the Federal Reserve during his lifetime.[69]

Based on actuarial tables, the Director of the National Economic Council ,who turns 72 this year, should last another 13 years or so. In other words, the president's top advisor on the economy is okay with zero-cost money through 2032. But who doesn't love easy money? Some observers do give credit where it is due. First,

---

69 "Kudlow: Fed may not hike interest rates 'in my lifetime."
https://www.politico.com/story/2019/04/11/larry-kudlow-
interest-rates-1269762. CAITLIN OPRYSKO, Politico 2019. Web.
11 April 2019.

easy money is great until you miss a payment or two.

Second, it was easy money that has already brought us two progressively worse Wall Street meltdowns and Main Street recessions so far this century, David Stockman former Director Office of Management and Budget under President Reagan, wrote to subscribers April 26, 2019. You know that could happen again, right. And the next time couldn't possibly be worse than the last two times, right. Of course it could.[70]

I have met Larry Kudlow along with many professionals who represent respectable companies. Goldman Sachs forecast no Fed rate hikes through the end of 2020. And Charles Evans, the president of the Chicago Fed, provided the 'money' quotes in reports from Bloomberg, Reuters, and the Wall Street Journal about a rate cut later this year.[71]

70 "The End of Bubble Finance Is Nigher Than You Think." https://www.deepstatedeclassified.com/dsd20190426/. David Stockman, Deep State Declassified 2019. Web. 26 April 2019.
71 "The End of Bubble Finance Is Nigher Than You Think." https://www.deepstatedeclassified.com/dsd20190426/. David Stockman, Deep State Declassified 2019. Web. 26 April 2019.

Global stocks have added $10 trillion in market capitalization so far this year, and our monetary central planners are here to keep it going, whether or not the "wealth effects" actually trickle down to Main Street. This stock market rally has everything, except investors. As The New York Times noted February 25, 2019, "Armchair investors have been selling stock." It's been companies that "keep buying huge quantities of their own shares, propelling prices higher even as pensions, mutual funds, and individuals sit on their hands.[72]

American corporations flush with cash from last year's tax cuts and a growing economy are buying back their own shares at an extraordinary clip. They have good reason: Buybacks allow them to return cash to shareholders, burnish key measures of financial performance and goose their share prices."

---

72 "This Stock Market Rally Has Everything, Except Investors." https://www.nytimes.com/2019/02/25/business/stock-market-buybacks.html?. Matt Phillips, New York Times 2019. Web, 25 Feb 2019.

Sober observers can see the fundamental shift in how the stock market is operating. Corporations have become the single largest source of demand for American stocks. It's not the Millennials. In the face of economic, international, and political uncertainty the buy-back binge has helped a bull market celebrate its 10th birthday.

The S&P 500 is up about 340 percent since March 2009. But few expect that kind of gain over the next decade. Increasing numbers of investors are motivated to protect their gains and to diversify unlike they ever have before beyond the traditional 60/40, stocks/bonds mix. "The S&P 500 fell 14 percent in the fourth quarter, and 9 percent in December alone. That was the worst monthly performance since February 2009, and badly shook investor confidence, according to The New York Times, February 25, 2019.[73]

73 "This Stock Market Rally Has Everything, Except Investors." https://www.nytimes.com/2019/02/25/business/stock-market-buybacks.html?. Matt Phillips, New York Times 2019. Web. 25 Feb 2019.

A February 2019 survey of Bank of America Merrill Lynch portfolio managers reported that those holding more money in cash than usual outnumbered their equity friendly cohorts by 44 percentage points. That's the biggest margin since January 2009. In sharp contrast, American companies fourth quarter 2018 bought an estimated $240 billion of their own shares, according to an analysis by the Goldman Sachs team that handles buybacks for major companies. "That's nearly 60% higher than during the same period in 2017," opined The New York Times.[74]

This year some analysts at Goldman Sachs contend corporations will be by far the largest buyer of shares. Traditional investors to include individuals, mutual funds, pensions, and endowments are expected to be net sellers. Investors have good reason to be nervous. And

---

74 "BofA: Investors remain bearish on economy despite stocks rallying." https://www.pionline.com/article/20190212/ ONLINE/190219967/bofa-investors-remain-bearish-on-economy-despite-stocks-rallying. JAMES COMTOIS, Pensions & Investments 2019, Web. 12 Feb 2019..

investors do not need to see the future to prepare for the good, the bad, and the unforeseen.

First, employ newer technology to help you determine how much market loss is acceptable to you. Second, add active management strategies where you can see a pattern that moved investors out of risk assets in a bad year, like 2008 and the same strategies moved money from cash back into risk assets in a good year, like 2009. Third, identify positions that have little if any correlation to the stock market.

By analogy, good tennis and volleyball players learn to play both sides of the net, with the sun in their eyes and the gusts of wind on the court.

The best economy ever?

My how things have changed. It the good old days, the stock market reflected the real-world economy and the profits businesses extracted from it. These days, that's no longer the case. The truth is, the "best economy ever" according to President Donald Trump, with trademark hyperbole, isn't really working for the stock market and really isn't working at all for ordinary Americans.

Let's put things in perspective. From the end of the first quarter of 2012 up to today's fresh all-time high on May 1, 2019, the S&P 500 Index has risen by 109.7%. Meanwhile, pre-tax corporate **profits declined** from an annual "run rate" of $2.20 trillion as of March 31, 2012, to $2.18 trillion as of December 31, 2018.[75]

The stock market got off to its best start in 13 years in 2019, but these nose bleed stock averages isn't a result of the work on Main Street. When we look at last Friday's GDP report on the first quarter, according to the Department of Commerce, the U.S. economy grew at an annualized rate of 3.2% over the three months ended March 31.[76] But this was a low-quality report. This reality show is the result of massive share buybacks, one-time tax law changes,

75 "https://www.deepstatedeclassified.com/dsd20190501/." The Magic of Another New All Time High. David Stockman, Deep State Declassified 2019. Web. 1 May 2019.
76 "U.S. Economy Grew at 3.2% Rate in First Quarter." https://www.wsj.com/articles/u-s-economy-grew-at-3-2-rate-in-first-quarter-11556281892. Harriet Torry, the Wall Street Journal 2019.

accounting games and a shift from smaller, unlisted companies. Real final private sales grew at a puny annualized rate of 1.3%. This could be the deepest decline in nearly a decade.[77]

David Stockman opined, "Consumer durables production virtually collapsed, falling at an annualized rate of 15%. That takes out all the gains since 2016. In fact, we're back to the late stages of the 2008–09 recession," on May 1, 2019. It's worth noting that Stockman is the former Director of the Office of Management and Budget under President Ronald Reagan. After leaving the White House, Stockman had a 20-year career on Wall Street. These days Stockman is not in the business of defending a POTUS, nor is he representing a brokerage firm.[78]

Stockman went on to say, "Here's more 'low quality,' fresh from Commerce on Monday: The steepest drawdown in the savings rate in six

77 "https://www.deepstatedeclassified.com/dsd20190501/." The Magic of Another New All Time High. David Stockman, Deep State Declassified 2019. Web. 1 May 2019.
78 "https://www.deepstatedeclassified.com/dsd20190501/." The Magic of Another New All Time High. David Stockman, Deep State Declassified 2019. Web. 1 May 2019.

years accounted for all of the 0.7% growth in consumer spending in March." Some observers, including this one, are convinced that the "best economy ever" is nothing than a debt-fueled sugar high.

Some economists got excited all over again when China's Statistics Ministry reported earlier this month that the Middle Kingdom's GDP growth for the first quarter was 6.4%. That beat a consensus forecast of 6.3%.[79]

Do you notice a pattern here? A simple Google search reveals that China "beats" by 0.1% practically every quarter.

Beijing sets the growth targets and filters them down through the party apparatus. That includes the giant state-controlled banks and industrial enterprises. From there, the government provides whatever it takes – new credit, fresh bribes, sometimes punishment, too

79 "https://www.deepstatedeclassified.com/dsd20190501/." The Magic of Another New All Time High. David Stockman, Deep State Declassified 2019. Web. 1 May 2019.

– to deliver the plan. It would appear America is learning from China.

Neither Active Management Nor Diversification guarantee against market loss or greater or more consistent returns.

16

The proof is in the planning

In America, we know how to spend but we don't know how to set aside for the future. It was my pleasure talking to Gabriana from WMAP where we discussed how Investor's Advantage helps people set up goals and stay on track.

Here are some topics we discussed!

- Helping folks see their targets
- Knowing what kind of loss they're willing to accept
- My advice for the youth when it comes to finances

Since 1979, Investor's Advantage Corporation has been passionate about working with individuals who are looking to achieve financial independence. By proactively planning our clients' futures, we strive to develop attainable goals and achievable personal benchmarks. At Investor's Advantage Corporation we pride ourselves on our ability to build financial independence and confidence. We do this by creating transparent and efficient portfolios that strive to exceed client objectives.

When President John Grace founded Investor's Advantage Corporation in Westlake Village, California, he resolved to not take the same old Investment Approach as many companies in the "Financial Planning" industry. As one of the firms in Conejo Valley paying for independent research, Investor's Advantage works based on mathematical probabilities that relate to our client's specific financial positions within the scope of the entire global financial marketplace. This independent research is one of the cornerstones of our Investment Strategy that helps investors see the larger picture to make appropriate and informed decisions.

17

FROM COMPLACENCY TO PANIC IN A NANOSECOND

The coronavirus has made its way to the Western world, sparking fears of a global pandemic. Of concern is a new case in California where the patient hadn't come from a country known to have the virus. Which means the patient must have contacted an infected person within the United States, implying there could be many more infected people at large. As I'm writing this message, I see that a second coronavirus case of unknown origin is confirmed in California, indicating the virus is spreading in the state, according to the *Washington Post*. News of the spreading virus triggered a massive selloff in the markets. The S&P 500 fell 10% in just six days, per Yahoo Finance. The markets are clearly in correction territory. This could just be the beginning.[80]

What a difference a week makes. With new infections occurring at a higher rate outside of China than inside the country, investors are understandably concerned that the coronavirus will severely cut global GDP. Chinese suppliers are running low on inventory and can't get workers back to the factory. Italy canceled the famous Venice Festival and is warning against people congregating in public places. It might be good for Netflix and food delivery companies, but this one looks like it's going to hurt.

Starting last month, this adviser has been stating in client meetings, and across the country in TV and radio news interviews, 2020 feels eerily similar to 2000. Like then, everything

80 "What Happens After the SPX Hits Correction Territory." https://finance.yahoo.com/news/happens-spx-hits-correction-territory-130000581.html. Rocky White Schaeffer's Investment Research, Yahoo Finance 2020. Web. 4 March 2020.

everywhere was hitting new highs in January. But starting February 2000, the NASDAQ, thanks to the tech wreck, lost 80% of its value after quadrupling from 1995–2000, according to Yahoo Finance. With $100k in tech stocks, mid-decade investors finished 1999 with about $400k. Starting in February 2000, the correction took tech stocks down by 80%, leaving those investors with about $80k, according to Yahoo Finance. What a ride.[81]

Last year investors worried about the effects of President Trump's Trade War. This year the coronavirus has erupted, causing investors to worry about how bad things can get. There's a notorious saying on Wall Street that the stock market takes the stairs up and the elevator down.

I'm fond of saying: it's not about the prediction, it's all about the preparation. No one saw the bus called coronavirus coming for us. And no one needed to see that one either. For some time I

81 "Current Equities Rally Similarities To 1999."
https://finance.yahoo.com/news/current-equities-rally-similarities-1999-152243773.html. Chris Vermeulen FX Empire, Yahoo Finance 2019. Web. 19 December 2019.

have agreed with Former Office of Management & Budget Director under President Reagan, David Stockman, that underneath the surface, there is a financial malignancy that's devouring the very foundations of capitalist prosperity in America.

In fact, I have come to know David Stockman thanks to paying—starting in 1999—to become a Master Certified and Charter Member at Dent Research. Research that is objective and independent has been beneficial to us, as we prepare our clients for the good, the bad, and the unforeseen.

Buy and hold works just fine when you don't need the money. Buy the dip can work too when you have fresh cash to add to your portfolio. But savvy investors hate losses more than they love gains. This is especially true when investors need to take money out to live or must take rising income every year for the rest of their lives to satisfy IRS Required Minimum Distributions from traditional retirement accounts. While the industry has taught investors to buy and hold, no matter what, savvy investors hate losses more than they love gains.

Savvy investors do the math. If you were 70 ½ in January 2008 with $1 million in your IRA invested in stocks, you might have fully participated in the serious 60% drawdown by March 2009. After the 57% market loss and a modest 3% (to keep the math easy) withdrawal, what was $1 million in January 2008 becomes $400k in no time at all. Now you need a 160% gain just to get back to even. Clearly, the odds of getting back to your high watermark are not in your favor. And you know you must increase your withdrawal rate for the rest of your life. You must sell part of what you have. Every year. Forever.

Instead of insulting investors with an approach that feels like a "Sit and take it," we employ technology and take the time to help you

1. Discover, perhaps for the first time, how much loss can you accept

2. Design the portfolio, and give it the attention the job deserves, to see if the account may perform within your personalized loss parameters.

3. Apply active management strategies to portfolios to help limit loss. Instead of holding shares and watch the price go down like the Titanic, your money is looked at daily with this question. Should coal be put on this fire to enjoy the melt-up, or is water better at this time to limit the melt-down?

4. Add more investment legs to your portfolio stool. We will offer different vehicles that have little or

no correlation to the stock market.

Sometimes boring trumps excitement.

No central monetary planner is omnipotent. We continue to be nimble and fact-driven. We understand there's a time to make money and a time to keep the money. If you have any questions about your holdings, please give us a call.

All investments involve the risk of potential investment losses and no strategy can assure a profit.. Neither asset allocation, active management, nor diversification guarantee against market loss or greater or more consistent returns. Securities America and its representatives do not provide tax advice; therefore, it is important to coordinate with your tax advisor regarding your specific situation. An investor cannot invest directly in an index. Past performance does not guarantee future results.

References

1 "2019 Retirement Pulse Survey." https://s2.q4cdn.
   com/437609071/files/doc_news/research/2019/
   retirement-pulse-survey.pdf. 2019. PDF File.

2 Markets Insider. 20 Feb. 2019. https://markets.
   businessinsider.com/news

3 "DoubleLine's Gundlach says new U.S. tariffs on China
   likely." https://finance.yahoo.com/news/doublelines-
   gundlach-says-u-tariffs-173249134.html. Reuters,
   Yahoo Finance 2019. Web. 7 May 2019.

4 Trish Reagan . "Interview: Trish Regan of Fox Business
   News Interviews Donald Trump." 2018. Video.

5-6 "Core Fixed Income & Flexible Income." https://
   doublelinefunds.com/webcasts/#. Jeffrey Gundlach,
   2019 2019. Web. 14 May 2019.

7 "DoubleLine's Gundlach says new U.S. tariffs on China
   likely." https://finance.yahoo.com/news/doublelines-
   gundlach-says-u-tariffs-173249134.html. Reuters,
   Yahoo Finance 2019. Web. 7 May 2019.

8 "When The Wall Street Chart-Monkeys Become
   Whirling Dervishes---It's Time For A Plan On How
   Not To Become COLLATERAL DAMAGE." https://
   davidstockmanscontracorner.com/when-the-wall-
   street-chart-monkeys-become-whirling-dervishes-its-
   time-for-a-plan-on-how-not-to-become-collateral-
   damage/. David Stockman, Contra Corner 2019. Web.
   15 May 2019.

9 Yahoo Finance. 2019. 2019. Web. 8 March 2019

10 https://www.cnn.com/business. 2015. Web. 9 March 2015

11 "Trump Proposes a Record $4.75 Trillion Budget." https://www.nytimes.com/2019/03/11/us/politics/trump-budget.html. Michael Tackett Jim Tankersley , 2019 2019. Web. 11 March 2019.

12 "The truth about Trump's 'economic miracle'." https://www.bostonglobe.com/opinion/2019/02/07/the-truth-about-trump-economic-miracle/dHaLjfw4y5A5nqv990c3AJ/story.html. Margery Eagan, 2019 2019. Web. 7 Feb 2019.

13-14 "Wall Street mulls sub-2% U.S. growth as consumers cut back on spending." https://finance.yahoo.com/news/wall-street-economic-gdp-growth-less-than-2-percent-155133619.html. Javier E. David, Yahoo Finance 2019. Web. 11 March 2019.

15 "We're at the high end of fair market value, says Vanguard chief investment officer." https://www.cnbc.com/video/2019/02/11/were-at-the-high-end-of-fair-market-value-says-vanguard-president.html. SQUAWK ALLEY, 2019 2019. Web. 11 Feb 2019.

16-18 "Majority of young workers have already tapped their retirement savings." https://www.cnbc.com/2018/08/21/millennials-and-early-401k-withdrawals.html. Sarah O'Brien, 2018 2018. Web. 21 Aug 2018.

19 "Investors Have Learned To Squat 10 Years After the Lehman Brothers Bankruptcy." https://www.thestreet.com/investing/investors-have-learned-squat-10-years-after-the-lehman-brothers-bankruptcy-14707453. BRIAN SOZZI, TheStreet 2018. Web. 11 Sep 2018.

20 "Pension Funds Pile on Risk Just to Get a Reasonable Return." https://www.wsj.com/articles/pension-funds-pile-on-the-risk-just-to-get-a-reasonable-return-1464713013. Timothy W. Martin, The Wall Street Journal 2016. Web. 11 Oct 2019.

21 "Scotiabank Profit Falls 12%, Hurt by Energy Loans." https://www.wsj.com/articles/scotiabank-profit-falls-12-hurt-by-energy-loans-1464695495?mod=searchresults&page=1&pos=3. Rita Trichur, Ben Dummett, The Wall Street Journal. 2016. Web. 11 Oct 2019.

22-23 "Investment return of 12.3% brings Yale endowment value to $29.4 billion." https://news.yale.edu/2018/10/01/investment-return-123-brings-yale-endowment-value-294-billion. Karen N. Peart, Yale News 2018. Web. 1 Oct 2018.

24-26 "Investors Have Learned To Squat 10 Years After the Lehman Brothers Bankruptcy." https://www.thestreet.com/investing/investors-have-learned-squat-10-years-after-the-lehman-brothers-bankruptcy-14707453. BRIAN SOZZI, TheStreet 2018. Web. 11 Sep 2018.

27-30 "Investment return of 11.3% brings Yale endowment value to $27.2 billion." https://news.yale.edu/2017/10/10/investment-return-113-brings-yale-endowment-value-272-billion. Tom Conroy, Yale News 2017. Web. 11 October 2019.

31 "Pension Funds Pile on Risk Just to Get a Reasonable Return." https://www.wsj.com/articles/pension-funds-pile-on-the-risk-just-to-get-a-reasonable-return-1464713013. Timothy W. Martin, The Wall Street Journal 2016. Web. 11 Oct 2019.

32-33 "ALAN GREENSPAN: The bull market is over, and investors should 'run for cover'." https://markets.businessinsider.com/news/stocks/stock-market-news-alan-greenspan-warns-investors-to-run-for-cover-2018-12-1027818871. Rebecca Ungarino, 2018 2018. Web. 18 Dec 2018.

34 "CFO Survey: Recession Likely by Year-End 2019." https://www.fuqua.duke.edu/duke-fuqua-insights/cfo-survey-december-2018. John Graham, 2018 2018. Web. 12 Dec 2018.

35 "Former Fed Chair Yellen says excessive corporate debt could prolong a downturn." https://www.cnbc.com/2018/12/11/janet-yellen-says-excessive-corporate-debt-could-prolong-a-downturn.html. Thomas Franck, CNBC 2018. Web. 10 Oct 2018..

36 "What To Do With Your Investments in This Market." https://economyandmarkets.com/markets/investments-to-do-this-market/. Harry Dent, 2018 2018. Web. 28 Dec 2018.

37-39 "What the Government Shutdown Reveals About Us." Corporate Counsel Men of Color. https://www.ccmenofcolor.org/what-the-government-shutdown-reveals-about-us/. Marc Jeffrey. 2019. Web. 4 Feb 2019.

40-42 "One Shutdown Lesson Is That Americans Need to Save More." https://www.bloomberg.com/opinion/articles/2019-01-28/shutdown-lesson-americans-need-to-save-more. Tyler Cowen, Bloomberg Opinion 2019. Web. 2 Feb 2019.

43 "The Conference Board Consumer Confidence Index Declined in March." Market Watch. https://www. marketwatch.com/press-release/the-conference-board-consumer-confidence-index-declined-in-march-2019-03-26. 2019. Web. 26 March 2019.

44-45 "Opinion: This bullish economic news is a warning for the stock market." https://www.marketwatch.com/ story/this-bullish-economic-news-is-a-warning-for-the-stock-market-2018-03-20. Mark Hulbert, Market Watch 2018. Web. 20 March 2018.

46 "Could Gold's Day in the Sun Be Upon Us?." https:// economyandmarkets.com/economy/golds-day-in-the-sun-coming-soon/. Harry Dent, Economy & Markets 2018. Web. 14 Feb 2018.

47 "Mark Cuban: 'There was blood in the street' — here's the way I'm hedging the market swings." https:// www.cnbc.com/2018/02/13/here-is-the-way-mark-cuban-hedged-the-market-meltdown.html. Matthew J. Belvedere, https://www.cnbc.com/2018/02/13/ here-is-the-way-mark-cuban-hedged-the-market-meltdown.html 2018. Web. 13 Feb 2018.

48 Evanmichael.com. 2018. Web. 3 April 2018.

49 "What you need to know on Wall Street today." https://finance.yahoo.com/news/know-wall-street-today-161755896.html. Olivia Oran, Yahoo Finance 2018. Web. 5 Jun 2018.

50 "History of bear markets since 1929." https:// finance.yahoo.com/news/history-bear-markets-since-1929-143729786.html. . Jade Scipioni, Yahoo Finance 2018. Web. 26 Dec 2018.

51 Evanmichael.com. 2018. Web. 3 April 2018.

52 Business Insider. 2018. Web 11 June 2018.

53 "Hallmark of an Economic Ponzi Scheme." https:// www.hussmanfunds.com/comment/mc180604/. . John P. Hussman, Ph.D., Hussman Funds 2018. Web. 12 June 2018.

54-55 "Corporate Profits Are Crushing Wages, And The Tax Cuts Aren't Helping." https://talkmarkets. com/content/economics--politics/corporate-profits-are-crushing-wages-and-the-tax-cuts-arent-helping?post=179292. Harry Dent, Talk Markets 2018. Web. 12 Jun 2018.

56 "The 'Melt Up' Is Officially Underway." https:// stansberryresearch.com/articles/the-melt-up-is-officially-underway-3. Steve Sjuggerud, Stansberry Research 2018. Web. 31 July 2018.

57 "The Difference Between Good Inflation and Bad Inflation." https://charlessizemore.tumblr.com/post/172040106091/the-difference-between-good-inflation-and-bad. Charles Sizemore, Charles Sizemore's Tumblr 2018. Web. 19 March 2018.

58-59 "Active management: Don't retire without it." http:// proactiveadvisormagazine.com/active-management-dont-retire-without-it/. Linda Ferentchak, Proactive Advisor Magazine 2018. Web. 18 July 2018.

60-61 "Trade war with China could hit California hard. Here's how.." https://www.sacbee.com/news/politics-government/article230342089.html. Phillip Reese, The Sacramento Bee 2019. Web. 14 May 2019.

62 "Big-screen TVs and other products you buy that may get more expensive because of a possible trade war with China." https://www.cnbc.com/2018/04/04/big-screen-tvs-and-other-products-you-buy-that-may-get-more-expensive-because-of-a-possible-trade-war-with-china.html. Evelyn Cheng, CNBC 2019. Web. 14 May 2019.

63 "Are we heading into a recession? Some CFOs think it could happen soon." https://finance.yahoo.com/news/heading-recession-cfos-think-could-100518329.html. Megan Henney, CNBC 2019. Web. 12 June 2019.

64 "Next global financial crisis will strike in 2020, warns investment bank JPMorgan." https://www.independent.co.uk/news/business/news/next-financial-crisis-2020-recession-world-markets-jpmorgan-a8540341.html. Peter Stubley, Independent 2018. Web. 12 June 2019.

65-66 "The 2020s Might Be The Worst Decade In U.S. History." https://www.forbes.com/sites/johnmauldin/2018/05/24/the-2020s-might-be-the-worst-decade-in-u-s-history/#4600566d48d3. John Mauldin, Forbes 2018. Web. 12 June 2019.

67-68 "Stockman: Economy Will Plunge Into a Recession Due to Trade War Escalation and Easy Money Policies." Dir. . Perf. David Stockman . CNBC, 2019. Video.

69   "Kudlow: Fed may not hike interest rates 'in my lifetime." https://www.politico.com/story/2019/04/11/larry-kudlow-interest-rates-1269762. CAITLIN OPRYSKO, Politico 2019. Web. 11 April 2019.

70-71   "The End of Bubble Finance Is Nigher Than You Think." https://www.deepstatedeclassified.com/dsd20190426/. David Stockman, Deep State Declassified 2019. Web. 26 April 2019.

72-73   "This Stock Market Rally Has Everything, Except Investors." https://www.nytimes.com/2019/02/25/business/stock-market-buybacks.html?. Matt Phillips, New York Times 2019. Web. 25 Feb 2019.

74   "BofA: Investors remain bearish on economy despite stocks rallying." https://www.pionline.com/article/20190212/ONLINE/190219967/bofa-investors-remain-bearish-on-economy-despite-stocks-rallying. JAMES COMTOIS, Pensions & Investments 2019. Web. 12 Feb 2019.

75   "https://www.deepstatedeclassified.com/dsd20190501/." The Magic of Another New All Time High. David Stockman, Deep State Declassified 2019. Web. 1 May 2019.

76   "U.S. Economy Grew at 3.2% Rate in First Quarter." https://www.wsj.com/articles/u-s-economy-grew-at-3-2-rate-in-first-quarter-11556281892. Harriet Torry, the Wall Street Journal 2019.

77-79   "https://www.deepstatedeclassified.com/dsd20190501/." The Magic of Another New All Time High. David Stockman, Deep State Declassified 2019. Web. 1 May 2019.

80   "What Happens After the SPX Hits Correction Territory." https://finance.yahoo.com/news/happens-spx-hits-correction-territory-130000581.html. Rocky White Schaeffer's Investment Research, Yahoo Finance 2020. Web. 4 March 2020.

81   "Current Equities Rally Similarities To 1999." https://finance.yahoo.com/news/current-equities-rally-similarities-1999-152243773.html. Chris Vermeulen FX Empire, Yahoo Finance 2019. Web. 19 December 2019.

About the Author

John Grace, a Registered Principal with Securities America, Inc., is a professional with over 30 years of experience. John, an Eagle Scout, attended Carleton College in Minnesota, and is a former President and Trustee of the Ventura County Council of the Boy Scouts of America; a former Board Member and Finance Committee Member of the El Camino College Foundation in Torrance; a former Trustee of the California Lutheran Educational Foundation at California Lutheran University in Thousand Oaks; a former Charter Member of the American Heart Association Ventura County

Chapter; a past Executive Board Member of the Westlake Village Chamber of Commerce; and Past President of the Rotary Club of Westlake Village Sunrise.

Due to his Knowledge and experience, John is a frequent lecturer on financial matters and has been retained to conduct workshops for colleagues, corporations, and various colleges, universities, and adult education programs, in addition to participating as a regular Keynote Speaker for Junior Achievement events around Southern California.

For more information visit:WhyBePoor.com